college vegetarian cooking

COLLEGE Vegetarian COOKING

FEED YOURSELF AND YOUR FRIENDS

Megan Carle and Jill Carle

Photography by Penny De Los Santos

TEN SPEED PRESS

Published in the United States by Ten Speed Press, an imprint of the
Crown Publishing Group, a division of Random House, Inc., New York.
www.crownpublishing.com
www.tenspeed.com

Ten Speed Press and the Ten Speed Press colophon are registered
trademarks of Random House, Inc.

Library of Congress Cataloging-in-Publication Data

Carle, Megan.
  College vegetarian cooking : feed yourself and your friends / Megan Carle and Jill Carle ;
photography by Penny de los Santos.
      p. cm.
  Includes index.
  ISBN-13: 978-1-58008-982-1 (pbk.)
  ISBN-10: 1-58008-982-8 (pbk.)
  1. Vegetarian cookery. 2. Vegan cookery. I. Carle, Jill. II. Title.
  TX837.C345 2009
  641.5'636--dc22
                          2008043147
ISBN: 978-1-58008-982-1

Printed in China

Design by Betsy Stromberg
Food and prop styling by Jenny Martin-Wong

10 9 8 7 6 5 4 3 2

First Edition

contents

introduction

"It's not easy being green." I bet Kermit didn't know he was speaking on behalf of vegetarians everywhere, but he was. People are much more aware today than they were even ten years ago about vegetarian and veganism—so it all seems a lot less weird to most people. But it's still a way of eating that takes time and energy, and the willingness to educate yourself about nutrition and, sometimes, to stick up for your choices. It can feel like a lot of work. So we developed the recipes in this book to help you keep your food low-stress, delicious, and fun. Our goal was to focus on leaving out the meat without leaving out the taste, and after several rounds of recipe testing, our guinea pigs—most of whom were not vegetarians—just kept coming back for more.

Come to think of it, it's not so easy just plain feeding yourself. Even if you cooked before you left home, like we did, cooking on your own is going to be different than what you're probably used to. Believe us. As sisters, we started learning to cook in our family kitchen when we were kids. And then we went off to college. And graduate school. We learned quickly what it's like to cook on a hot plate with one busted pot, after having scrounged for grocery money under the couch cushions. Okay, slight exaggeration, but we definitely found that having less equipment, fewer dishes, and way less money to spend on food affects the way you cook and the kinds of things you cook. That's one of the reasons we wrote this book.

We also wrote it because we noticed how easy it is for students who don't have much money or confidence in the kitchen to get into really boring and not-so-healthy patterns of eating—even vegetarians (ramen, anyone?). The good news is that, since you're one of more than twelve million Americans who don't eat meat, you have a ton of cheap, tasty, healthy options, from good old cheese and pasta to soymilk to "superfoods" like broccoli and quinoa. (What's quinoa? Glad you asked! Check out pages 51 and 128.) Vegetarian cooking is no harder to learn or do than any other kind of cooking, and even beginners can whip out veggie comfort food (real mac and cheese), fast food (pizza, wraps), simple food (stir-fries), impressive food (fondue!), and decadent food (mmmm, dessert . . .) with just a little direction.

So this book aims to set you up with the basic skills and knowledge you'll need to get started, and to help you stay out of the baked potato rut (because seriously, who doesn't love a good spud, but not every day, okay?). If you know nothing about cooking, we'll teach you something. If you have some kitchen chops and some favorite dishes, we'll share more with you.

The first pages of the book have an overview of the ingredients and equipment we feel are essential to setting up a rudimentary vegetarian kitchen, and some of the basic skills and techniques you'll need there (cooking rice and pasta, for example). This is a good place to start if in the past you've mostly thought of the kitchen as the place where the frozen fudge pops are stored. Helpful shopping, prepping, cooking, and storing advice (and also some fun trivia) is scattered throughout the book in headnotes and sidebars. Because we know the likelihood of you sitting down to dinner at six o'clock every night is practically nonexistent, we categorized the recipes a little differently than in most cookbooks, which tend to group things by ingredient (beans, vegetables) or course (soup, salad). If you would have trouble making something suitable for yourself, let alone for other people, there's Survival Cooking: recipes that are very simple and won't strain your cooking abilities the first time out. When money is particularly tight, check out the Cheap Eats chapter, where you'll find great dishes that are very budget friendly (though really, nearly every recipe is written with economy in mind). For those weeks when you've overindulged, check out Avoiding the Freshman Fifteen. It's full of recipes that are so good you won't feel the least bit deprived. Knowing that students often fly solo for meals led us to the Dinner for One chapter. Not only are these single-portion recipes great for those cooking for themselves, but they also give you an option to make your own meatless dinner when everyone else in your apartment is eating pot roast. And some of them have the option of making enough for dinner tonight and lunch tomorrow. For those times when you need a little TLC, check out the comfort food in Just Like Mom Makes. It's like being home . . . without being told to get your elbows off the table. We've also included a couple of chapters that will help you feed your friends. Food for the Masses offers hearty dishes that will serve eight to twelve people, and Party Food is, well, food to take to a party (go figure). As easy as it is to be the one who always brings the loaf of French bread and cheese, this gives you an opportunity to try something a little more interesting. And once you have won over your friends by cooking for them (see how this can be really good for your social life?), you'll be more than ready to start thumbing through the Impressing Your Date chapter. Because nothing says I Really Like You like a plateful of Mushroom Ravioli in Browned Butter. As for the last chapter—well, you have to have Desserts, right? 'Nuff said.

kitchen basics

H ere are some basics about ingredients, equipment, and cooking techniques that you should know before starting in on the recipes. We don't explain this stuff throughout the book because it comes up a lot and so it makes more sense to keep it in one place. You'll probably want to refer back here often.

Ingredients

Bouillon: This is basically dehydrated vegetable stock, and it's a key component to making sure your soups and sauces have good, full flavor. In this book, we used bouillon cubes instead of stock or broth because they're cheaper and a lot lighter to carry home from the store. The only size of vegetable bouillon cubes we found are extra large and are dissolved in 2 cups of water. If you find regular-sized ones, just use two for every one we call for. If you are using broth or stock, just substitute that for the water called for in the recipe (and leave out the bouillon cube, of course). No-salt-added vegetable bouillon cubes are a great option if your store carries them. They contain about 10 percent of the sodium of regular cubes, but still deliver all the flavor.

Breadcrumbs: We use plain breadcrumbs, but it's not that big of a deal for any of the dishes in this book. If what you have on hand is seasoned, don't make a special trip to the store; they'll work fine. Or if you don't have any at all, place a few slices of bread in the oven at 250°F for 20 minutes, or until they are dried out. Cool completely and break the slices into half-inch pieces. Place in the blender and pulse until smooth.

Butter: We've always used salted butter. It used to be because that's what Mom bought, but now it's because we prefer salted butter to use on bread and it's too much hassle to buy both kinds. If you prefer unsalted, you may need to add a little extra salt to the recipes.

Margarine can be substituted for butter in all of the recipes in this book. Substituting can often be a problem with desserts, but we made all of these vegan so you wouldn't have to worry about it. We use stick margarine rather than soft; choose a brand that is free of trans fats.

Cooking spray and oil: Fat's got a bad rep, but some fat is part of a healthy diet (your brain especially needs healthy fats to function well). Also, you often need it to cook with. We usually say butter or spray the pan in recipes. We always spray. It's faster, you don't have to get your hands all greasy, and it's much lower in fat, and therefore calories. We use plain, unflavored cooking spray—which is just cooking oil and an emulsifier in an aerosol can or pump bottle—and since we're paying for it now, we buy the store brand. It's cheaper and it works just as well as name-brand products. Canola, corn, or vegetable oils are good to cook with: its flavor is neutral. If you want to cook with olive oil, the plain, nonfancy stuff will do—save the extra virgin olive oil for salad dressing. And for future reference, olive oil is not a substitute for canola oil, especially in dessert recipes. Brownies with olive oil are really gross. Ask my roommate.

Cornstarch: If you make a lot of stir-fries, you'll want cornstarch on your shelf. It is a fast and easy way to thicken sauces, but it can cause a real mess if it's not used properly. It must be mixed with a little bit of cold liquid before being added to the sauce or whatever; otherwise, it will immediately form large lumps that will never smooth out. You don't need a lot of liquid, just enough to form a smooth, pourable mixture. One other tip about cornstarch: It doesn't have much staying power when it's used in a sauce. It's meant to be used right before serving. If it cooks for more than 10 minutes, your sauce will begin to thin out again. Cornstarch is also used a lot to thicken the filling for fruit pies—you'll use it if you make the peach pie in chapter 9, for instance.

Fruits and vegetables: Organic or not organic—that is the question. Whether 'tis better to suffer the slings and arrows of nasty pesticides or to blow six bucks on two peaches. . . . Oh, sorry. They made us take a Shakespeare class freshman year. But really, what is a broke vegetarian supposed to do? We know the benefits of organics (better for the environment, better for your health, taste better), but they can be totally beyond reach, price-wise. The truth is, some conventionally grown (that is, nonorganic) fruits and vegetables are grown with lots of chemicals, some with hardly any. If this is really important to you, and you can afford some organics, go for organic apples, cherries, spinach, celery, and berries. Fruits or vegetables you peel (like carrots or bananas or peas) and broccoli and cauliflower don't expose you to as many chemicals, so buy those organic if cost is no object (yeah, right). Likewise, farmer's markets, which happen in most towns at least once a week (closing for the winter in cold climates), can be really inspiring but really expensive places to shop for produce. It's great to be able to give your food money right to the people who grew it, and you should definitely check out your local farmer's market if you haven't already. The vendors will entice you with samples, and in the height of the growing season, prices can be really competitive. For bargains, try going near the end of the market day and asking for a discount—growers would often rather sell their stuff for cheap than pack it back up and take it home.

For those times when fresh fruits and vegetables aren't available or you just don't have the time to deal with them, the canned or frozen versions are generally good alternatives. Whether you use frozen or canned is up to you. In these recipes we used the one we felt worked best in each situation, but feel free to use whichever one you prefer.

Herbs and spices: We use dried herbs more often than fresh herbs in our recipes simply because they're cheaper and easier to have on hand. When we use fresh herbs, it's because the dish needs the slightly different flavor that the fresh herb provides. Dried herbs are usually more potent than their fresh counterparts. That said, now we'll tell you why it isn't always true. In general, dried herbs are more potent than fresh for the first three months. Once that time has passed they begin to lose their potency, and after six months their flavoring power drops dramatically. The same holds true with spices. Manufacturers recommend replacing dried herbs and spices every six months. Since that isn't feasible on our budget, we just taste each dish and add more if it seems like the herb or spice has lost its punch.

Lemon juice: Freshly squeezed lemon juice has a fresher flavor than the bottled version, but we still always keep a bottle of lemon juice in the refrigerator. If we plan ahead, we buy fresh lemons. But if we don't have fresh ones on hand, we aren't likely to go to the store just to get them.

Margarine: see Butter.

Mayonnaise, yogurt, and sour cream: Generally, we use light or low-fat versions, because we are all for saving a few calories when we can't taste the difference. Just keep in mind that low-fat versions tend to get watery when they are mixed with other ingredients. So, if you are making something to eat right away, the low-fat mayo is fine, but if you want to serve it later, mix in the mayo right before serving. (And by the way, we say mayonnaise, but we actually use Miracle Whip. That's what Mom always bought and that's what we're used to. Use whichever one you prefer.) Low-fat or even nonfat plain yogurt is a fine substitute for whole-fat—especially if you can find Greek or European-style plain nonfat yogurt—it's been drained of extra water, so it's really creamy.

Mushrooms: Fresh mushrooms should be brushed off, rinsed briefly under running water, and patted dry with a paper towel. Never soak them in water; they are like little sponges and will absorb water and become soggy. Also, be sure to trim off the ends (the part that would stick in the ground) before you use them.

Piecrust: Premade piecrusts are wonderful and way easier than making your own. The kind we buy are in the refrigerator section and usually come in boxes with two crusts. It is best to let them sit until they're room temperature because otherwise they crack when you try to unroll them. If you're impatient like me you can throw them in the microwave for a few seconds, but don't put them in for too long or they'll stick together.

Potatoes: There are many different types of potatoes available in the store, but we usually use red or russets (also called Idaho). Red potatoes are more expensive than russets, but they are also less starchy. Since they hold their shape better when sliced, we always use them for potato salads. For almost everything else we use russet potatoes. They are cheap and work well for baking, mashing, or frying.

Puff pastry and phyllo dough: We are huge fans of frozen dough. It is easy to use and makes you look like a pro. In most grocery stores you'll find them in the freezer section by the desserts. Just be sure to thaw them in the refrigerator (think ahead: it takes about 8 hours). If you thaw them at room temperature, the condensation will make the dough sticky and hard to work with.

Rice: With long-grain, short-grain, medium-grain, white, brown, and more, the variety of different types of rice can be overwhelming. The good news is that any of those will work in these recipes. Beyond size and shape, the difference between long-, medium-, and short-grain rice is the amount of starch released during cooking. Short-grain rice releases a lot of starch and is sticky when cooked. Long-grain releases much less starch and is fluffy when cooked. White and brown rice start out the same, but white rice has the nutritious, high-fiber bran coating removed. Because brown rice still has the bran coating, it takes 20 to 25 minutes longer to cook. Rice used in sushi is a type of Japanese short-grained white rice that has the right amount of starch to be sticky, but not mushy. It's best to stick with rice that's specifically labeled sushi rice if you want your sushi rolls to stay together. Jasmine rice is a long-grained Thai rice that has a kind of nutty flavor and is often used in Asian or Indian dishes. It's not as sticky as other rice and is good for adding that extra flavor. Armed with all that information, you can choose whichever type you like, but truth be told, we buy whichever one is cheapest.

Size matters: All eggs in the recipes are large. All other ingredients are medium unless we mention a size. In other words, if we just say potato, we mean a medium-sized potato. If we say large potato, we mean a large potato. Just don't get carried away. If it's big enough to make you say, "Wow, look at that!" it's too big.

Soy products: For vegetarians and vegans alike, soybeans and their derivatives can provide a good source of protein that you don't get from meat. Products containing soy protein appear in nearly every aisle of the supermarket. That's because soy doesn't just mean tofu. Traditional soy foods also include soymilk, soynuts, and edamame (green soybeans), just to name a few. Soy is a versatile bean used mostly in Asia and is found in foods like soymilk, soy sauce, miso (soybean paste), tempeh (see page 48), and tofu (see page 15). Soy is also sometimes added to foods like breads, cereals, and meat products, and used as a meat substitute in products such as soy burgers and soy hot dogs.

In *College Vegetarian Cooking*, we often use tofu, which comes in a variety of forms. Silken tofu is a softer form of tofu that is also known as Japanese-style tofu; it can be used to make vegan salad dressings, puddings, and a variety of other dishes that require a smooth consistency. Regular firm tofu, also known as Chinese tofu, is better suited for stir-frying because it maintains its form. Baked and flavored tofus allow you to skip the marinating process, giving more flavor in less time. Although we do not use soymilk or soy cheese very often in this book, if you are a vegan you of course can substitute anything you wouldn't eat for the corresponding vegan product.

Techniques

Cooking asparagus: The ends of asparagus should be broken off, not cut. Hold the stem end in one hand and about 2 inches below the tip in the other. Bend the asparagus and break off the end. It may seem that you're discarding more than you should, but what you're throwing away is the tough portion that isn't pleasant to eat. Cook asparagus in the same manner as broccoli, checking it often. It should be soft, not mushy.

Cooking broccoli: Broccoli is a vegetable that seems to cause people trouble. This one's easy: just don't overcook it. Place the broccoli in a pan with about 1 inch of water. Bring the water to a boil, cover, and cook over medium-high heat for 4 minutes. Check for tenderness and cook for 1 to 2 more minutes if necessary. Broccoli should be bright green and tender but not soggy. Under no circumstances should broccoli ever be cooked for more than 7 minutes. After that, it loses its color and becomes soggy.

Cooking pasta: The key to making perfect pasta is a lot of boiling water. If you don't have enough water or the water isn't boiling when you put in the pasta, you'll end up with a large gelatinous mass. To cook 1 pound of pasta, use at least a 3-quart saucepan. Fill the pan

with water, add a teaspoon of salt, and bring the water to a full boil. Add the pasta and stir frequently as it cooks. The cooking time will depend on the thickness of the pasta; angel hair will take about 5 minutes, but linguine or penne could take up to 15 minutes. Pasta is usually cooked al dente, which literally translates as "to the tooth," meaning it should offer slight resistance when bitten into and not be overly soft. The easiest way to test for doneness is to remove one piece with a fork and taste it. If you're still not sure, you can use the super high-tech method of throwing it against the wall. If it sticks, it's done; if not, be more patient!

Cooking rice: For each cup of rice, use 2 1/4 cups of water. Place the water and rice in a small saucepan and bring to a boil over high heat. Cover and simmer over medium-low heat for 20 minutes, or until most of the water has been absorbed. You don't need to stir it, and you shouldn't take the cover off more than once or twice—this lets the steam escape. Remove from the heat and let stand for 5 minutes. Once you turn the heat off, the rice will soak up a little bit more water, but don't count on that. If there's still quite a bit of water in the bottom, keep the heat on. Brown rice is cooked the same way, except it needs to simmer for about 45 minutes.

Frying with oil: There are entire books written about kitchen safety, but the issue we feel compelled to mention here is that oil and water don't mix. Whenever you're frying something in oil, be sure to use a pan that is at least twice the depth of the oil. This allows room for the oil to bubble up without running over the sides of the pan. Also, make sure that the food you're adding is as dry as possible. We know that it's impossible for everything you fry to be completely dry, but it isn't hard to avoid excess liquids. In the unlikely event that you do start a grease fire, do not use water to put it out. Water will make the oil spatter, spreading the fire. Sprinkling baking soda on the fire should put it out. As for all the different cooking terms—frying, sautéing, stir-frying—it all depends on heat and fat. (We know. Super appealing . . .) Frying involves very hot temperatures and a considerable amount of oil or fat. Sautéing uses less oil and moderately high temperatures to brown food while keeping all the flavor. Stir-frying is done at very high temperatures with just a little oil. This is usually done in a wok—though you can use a big skillet or frying pan, too—and stirred continuously, hence "stir-frying."

Peeling garlic: Smash the garlic clove by placing it on a flat surface, laying the blade of a large knife flat on top of the garlic, and hitting the knife with the heel of your hand. Remove and discard the papery skin and finely chop the garlic.

Storing and washing produce: Storing your fruits and veggies the wrong way can ruin them before you get a chance to eat them. What's the right way? That depends. Here are some quick rules of thumb:

1. Almost everything can go in the fridge in plastic bags except for bananas, tomatoes, citrus, and potatoes. Keep those at cool room temperature.

2. Things that keep the longest: apples, potatoes, onions, garlic, citrus.

3. Things that go bad fast: fresh herbs, eggplant, asparagus, soft berries.

Some vegetables are pickier than others and don't play nice with the other vegetables. For example, onions and potatoes should not be stored together because they spoil faster. Regardless of whether you buy organic or conventionally grown produce, wash or peel all fruits and vegetables before using them. But don't wash produce as soon as you get it home, and then store it—any moisture left over from the washing process can make it spoil faster. There's nothing much sadder than finding a bag of disintegrating lettuce goo where your salad greens should have been. Plain running water and some rubbing with your fingers gets rid of most dirt and germs. For leafy greens like lettuce and spinach, plunge them into a bowl of water and swirl them around to gently wash off the dirt (you might have to do this a few times with unbagged spinach, which brings a good chunk of mud along with it from the field), then shake in a colander and dry thoroughly with paper or kitchen towels or dry in a salad spinner. Or if your budget can stand it, buy bagged prewashed greens. Veggie washes, which you can buy in the produce department, are a waste of money. Water and friction should do the trick. But if you want to, you can make your own veggie wash by splashing a little vinegar (any kind) into a cup of water and then rubbing that over your produce (then rinsing) or swirling it in your lettuce-rinsing water.

Tools and Equipment

The following are basic items you should have to cook the dishes in this book (and most others, too). The first section is a list of items we think are essential; the second section lists things that aren't necessary but will sure make life easier. It may seem like a lot of stuff, but we aren't talking about top-of-the-line brands here. If you head to the local discount or thrift store, you should be able to get everything you need for right around $100.

You don't need to buy everything at once. You can get the basics right away and fill in the rest as you go along. Better yet, you can give the list to your mom as a birthday or holiday list. If your mom is anything like ours, you'll end up with everything on the list, and it will be better quality than anything you would buy yourself.

NECESSARY ITEMS

Pots and pans: These usually come in eight-piece sets that include a 1-quart covered saucepan (that's the deepish round one with a handle), a 2-quart covered saucepan, a 5-quart covered stockpot (you'll cook pasta and soups in here), and two skillets. They vary greatly in price, running anywhere from

$15 into the hundreds of dollars. While your immediate reaction may be to go for the $15 set, they aren't much stronger than aluminum foil and won't last too long before the handles fall off. The sets that cost around $50 are decent and will last you through college, as long as you aren't on the eight-year plan.

Knives: Take it from someone who knows, having one steak knife grows old quickly. It would be ideal to have one of those six- or eight-piece sets, but all you truly need is a paring knife, a large (chef's) knife for chopping, and if you can afford it, a serrated knife for cutting bread. If you buy cheap knives, just remember that there's a reason they were cheap. You will probably spend longer than it's worth trying to cut up vegetables. Hint: It's not a good thing when the blade bends.

Baking pans: You will need to have one baking sheet (11 by 15 inches is a standard size, but make sure you have one that will fit in your oven), one 9 by 13-inch pan, and one 8-inch square pan. If you can afford it, it's handy to have two 9 by 13-inch pans and two baking sheets.

Blender: This is the only electrical appliance we use in this book (except for a microwave, which isn't required). You could probably live without a blender, but it's extremely helpful to have one. It doesn't need to be the mega model. We got one on sale at the grocery store for $13 and it works fine.

Stacking bowls: These are graduated bowls that come in plastic, glass, or metal. They're useful for cooking (you'll need them if you bake) and serving (use them for salad). At home we have glass, but we found a set of four plastic bowls at a discount store for $4, and they're fine.

Colander: Plastic or metal doesn't matter; just get one large enough to hold a pound of cooked pasta (about 3 quarts).

Can opener: Electric is nice, but handheld works just fine.

Spatulas: If you have nonstick pans, you'll need a plastic spatula so you don't ding up the nonstick surface, but metal spatulas are thinner and work better for taking cookies off of baking sheets and getting food out of baking pans intact. Buy one of each if you can afford it.

Measuring cups: It's best to have a set of stacking dry measuring cups and a 2-cup liquid measuring cup. If you can't afford both, buy the dry set.

Measuring spoons: Trust us on this one: buy a set with the measurements stamped into the metal or plastic. If the numbers are just printed on, they'll wash off after a while, and then you go nuts trying to figure out which one is which.

Other stuff: Aluminum foil and plastic wrap are essential for cooking and storing food—you should always have some on hand. Zip-top bags are also seriously useful; get the heavyweight ones if you are using them to store food in the freezer.

HELPFUL ITEMS

Large spoons: Either metal or wooden (wooden if your pans are nonstick). These will save you a ton of time you'd otherwise spend fishing out little spoons when they slide into a pan full of food.

Rubber scraper: Scrapers are helpful if you plan to do any baking. We like the ones made of soft rubber rather than hard plastic because they bend, making it easier to scrape everything out of the bowl.

Cutting board: Cutting on the counter will dull your knives and tick off your apartment manager. Get either wood or plastic, whichever you prefer. Both work fine.

Grater: This can save you a lot of time. We like the box graters with three different grating sides and one slicing side.

Garlic press: If you hate the smell of garlic on your hands, this is a must-have. It's so much faster and easier than peeling and chopping garlic.

Hot pads or oven mitts: These come in very handy. You can use a kitchen towel instead, but if the towel is even the least bit damp, you'll feel the heat immediately.

Pastry brushes: Again, these are not necessary, but they do come in handy. We use pastry brushes the most with pastries. (Who knew?) They're especially good for brushing dough with butter or egg whites, but they can also be used to baste food in the oven or on the grill. We bought a set of three for $1 at the dollar store.

Vegetable brush: A vegetable brush is a good investment if you eat lots of firm fruits and vegetables with their skins on (apples, potatoes). Buy a brush especially for this purpose—don't use your dish brush or scrubber. That's just gross.

Vegetable peeler: You can peel fruit and vegetables with a knife, but we say why bother? Vegetable peelers are so cheap it seems silly to hassle with a knife.

Stocking Your Pantry

There's nothing more frustrating than starting to cook something and then realizing you don't have all of the ingredients. This list won't stop that from happening, but it will help your chances of having what you need without having to run to the store. Of course, the best way to make sure you have what you need is to read the recipe's ingredients list in advance and check the fridge and pantry for what you have and what you'll need to buy.

The first section lists basic items you'll use frequently when you're cooking from this book and many others. The second section contains the essentials for making desserts (though some stuff you'll need for baking is in the first list, such as flour and white sugar). Personally, we think these belong with the necessary items, but you can decide for yourself.

WHAT EVERY KITCHEN SHOULD HAVE

Cooking spray	Salt	Pepper	Flour
Sugar	Cornstarch	Canola oil	Soy sauce
Lemon juice or lemons	Vegetable bouillon	Rice vinegar	White wine vinegar
Mexican seasoning	Italian seasoning	Ground ginger	Fresh garlic
Butter or margarine	Eggs	Milk	Pasta
Rice	Potatoes	Onions	Canned diced tomatoes
Parmesan cheese	Crushed red pepper	Curry powder	Chili powder
Canned beans			

BAKING ESSENTIALS

Baking soda	Baking powder	Brown sugar	Confectioner's sugar
Cinnamon	Vanilla		

survival cooking

1

black bean and corn soft tacos

j: We have two recipes for tacos in this book, which may seem repetitive, but the only similarity is the tortillas and cheese. This version has the great combo of black beans and corn, with a little bit of zip from the sauce. **Serves 4**

1/2 cup sour cream

1 (4-ounce) can hot green chiles

1 (15-ounce) can black beans

1 (15-ounce) can corn kernels

1 tablespoon chili powder

16 (6-inch) corn tortillas or
8 (8-inch) flour tortillas

1 1/2 cups shredded lettuce

1 cup grated Cheddar cheese

Combine the sour cream and green chiles in a small bowl and set aside.

Drain the beans, rinse under cold water, and place in a small saucepan. Add the corn and its liquid and cook over medium-low heat, stirring occasionally, for 8 to 10 minutes, or until hot. Drain the liquid and stir in the chili powder.

Place 4 corn tortillas or 2 flour tortillas on a plate. If you are using corn tortillas, double them up, so you have 2 stacks of 2 tortillas each. Spoon some of the black bean mixture onto the centers. Top with the lettuce, cheese, and sour cream sauce as desired. Repeat with the remaining ingredients.

Okay, let's just get this over with. We all know that beans are loaded with great nutrients and are low in fat. Unfortunately, we also know that they can cause . . . an embarrassing issue. So, what to do? If you're using canned beans, rinse them before you use them, like in this recipe. If you cook beans, soak them for a few hours first, then drain them. Use fresh water to cook them and cook until they're very soft. I've heard that this can lessen the effects by up to 80 percent.

food for thought

tomato tart

m: This tasty recipe is like pizza, but easier. It takes about 2 minutes to prepare, looks impressive, and tastes great. Puff pastry isn't used much in the United States, but Europeans can't do without it. It's really easy to work with, and the results are always perfect. To thaw frozen puff pastry, put it in the refrigerator the night before you want to use it. **Serves 4**

Cooking spray or oil

1 sheet frozen puff pastry, thawed (see page 5)

2 tablespoons spicy mustard

5 slices Swiss cheese (about 4 ounces total)

2 large tomatoes

1/2 teaspoon Italian seasoning

Preheat the oven to 400°F. Generously coat a baking sheet with cooking spray or oil.

Unfold the puff pastry sheet and place it on the prepared pan. Spread the mustard over the pastry, leaving a 3/4-inch margin all around the edges, and top with the Swiss cheese. Slice the tomatoes 1/4 to 3/8 inch thick, arrange them over the cheese, then sprinkle with the Italian seasoning. Bake for 30 to 40 minutes, or until the puff pastry is golden brown. Serve hot or at room temperature.

I've always wondered what makes the holes in Swiss cheese, so I decided a little research was in order. After reading quite a bit about the process, I will simply say that the holes are made by sizable bubbles of gas produced in the cheese-ripening process. Anything more than that falls under way too much information—unless you're studying biochemistry, that is.

food trivia

vegetable kung pao

m : Stir-frying is one of the quickest, easiest, and healthiest ways to cook, and this recipe is a great introduction. You don't need a wok or any other special equipment, just a regular old frying pan and a spatula or wooden spoon. Once you get this recipe down, you can add your own touches. More or less spice, different vegetables, more garlic or ginger, different sauces—the possibilities are endless! One word of caution with this and other stir-fries: if you add wet vegetables to hot oil, the oil will sputter and spit, so drain or pat excess water off your ingredients. **Serves 4**

$2^1/4$ cups plus $1^1/2$ tablespoons water

1 cup rice

1 teaspoon cornstarch

3 tablespoons soy sauce

1 tablespoon rice vinegar

1 tablespoon sugar

1 small onion

4 stalks celery

3 zucchini

3 cloves garlic

2 tablespoons canola oil

$1/2$ teaspoon crushed red pepper

1 (8-ounce) can sliced water chestnuts

1 cup whole peanuts

> **?** There are a lot of stories about where the name "Kung Pao" came from, but all agree the dish was named for someone important—apparently, this gives it prestige. Personally, I just like it because it has peanuts.
>
> **food trivia**

Place the $2^1/4$ cups water and rice in a small saucepan and bring to a boil over high heat. Cover and simmer over medium-low heat for 20 minutes, or until most of the water is absorbed. Remove from the heat and let stand for 5 minutes. Combine the cornstarch, remaining $1^1/2$ tablespoons water, soy sauce, rice vinegar, and sugar in a small bowl, stir until smooth, and set aside.

Peel the onion and cut into $1/2$-inch pieces. Trim and discard the ends of the celery and zucchini and cut into $1/2$-inch pieces. Peel and finely chop the garlic or pass it through a garlic press.

Place the oil in a large skillet over medium-high heat. Let the oil get hot but not smoking (it's right when a drop of water flicked onto the surface of the oil evaporates right away). Add the onion, celery, zucchini, and crushed red pepper and cook, stirring frequently, for 8 to 10 minutes, or until the vegetables just start to get soft. The stirring is so the ingredients don't stick and so they get cooked evenly. Add the garlic and water chestnuts and cook, stirring frequently, for 2 to 3 minutes, or until the vegetables are still firm but also a bit tender. Pour the sauce mixture into the pan and cook, stirring constantly, for 1 minute, or until the sauce thickens. Stir in the peanuts and take the pan off the heat immediately. Spoon some rice into the center of each of 4 plates and top with equal amounts of the hot vegetables and sauce.

tofu tetrazzini

j: In our family, this dish is usually made with chicken. Then Megan started trying to convince us that tofu was actually good. I tried it reluctantly, and I was kind of surprised to find that the tofu wasn't bad (shocking, I know). So even though I'm not a true tofu believer, this is pretty good, especially if you use baked tofu, which holds together when you cut it up much better than regular tofu does. **Serves 6**

Cooking spray or oil

1 pound uncooked spaghetti

1 (8-ounce) package baked tofu

2 (10.75-ounce) cans cream of mushroom soup

1/2 cup grated Parmesan cheese

1 (15-ounce) can sliced mushrooms

1/2 cup milk

1 teaspoon salt

1/2 teaspoon pepper

Preheat the oven to 350°F. Coat a 9 by 13-inch baking pan with cooking spray or oil.

Bring a large saucepan of salted water to a boil and add the spaghetti. Cook over medium-high heat, stirring occasionally, for 10 minutes, or until al dente. Drain the spaghetti in a colander.

Meanwhile, cut the tofu into bite-size pieces and place in the baking pan. Add the cream of mushroom soup, Parmesan cheese, mushrooms with their juice, milk, salt, and pepper and stir well. Add the spaghetti and toss until it's completely coated and the tofu and mushrooms are fairly evenly distributed. Bake, uncovered, for 30 to 40 minutes, or until lightly browned. Remove from the oven and serve immediately.

Tofu can be purchased in different forms, including silken, regular, and baked. Silken tofu is soft and falls apart easily, but it gets very smooth when you purée it, making it good for sauces, dressings, and desserts. Regular tofu comes in soft, firm, and extra-firm types; the firm and extra-firm slice well and are good for baking or a stir-fry, where you want it to keep its shape. Baked tofu is regular tofu that has been marinated and baked, lowering its water content and making it substantially firmer. It comes in different flavors and is so delicious that you can just warm it up and eat it as is. If a recipe doesn't call for a specific type of tofu, stick with regular firm tofu.

cooking 101

pasta primavera

j: This is probably one of the easiest things you will ever make; plus, it gives you an opportunity to try new vegetables. If there are certain vegetables in season or on sale, just substitute those or include them along with the vegetables in the recipe. **Serves 4 to 6**

1 carrot

1 cup broccoli florets

1 small onion

1 zucchini

1 yellow squash

3 cloves garlic

1 large tomato

$1/2$ cup frozen peas

1 pound uncooked pasta

2 tablespoons olive oil

$1/2$ cup milk

$1/2$ cup grated Parmesan cheese, plus extra for sprinkling

Salt and pepper

Place a large saucepan with 1 inch of water over high heat and bring to a boil. Peel the carrot and cut into thin slices. Add the carrot slices and broccoli to the pan, cover, and cook for 4 minutes, or until the broccoli is still crisp but also a bit tender. Drain the water and set the broccoli and carrots aside. (Alternatively, if you have a microwave, place the carrots and broccoli in a microwave-safe container and add a little water. Cover with plastic wrap or wax paper and microwave on high heat for 5 minutes, or until tender.)

Peel the onion and cut into $1/2$-inch pieces. Cut the zucchini and yellow squash in half lengthwise, and then cut into thin slices. Peel and finely chop the garlic or put it through a garlic press. Cut the tomato in half, remove the seeds by scraping them out of the tomato with a small tool or your finger, and chop into $1/2$-inch pieces.

Place the peas in a colander. Fill the same large saucepan about two-thirds full with salted water, return it to the stove over high heat, and bring to a boil. Add the pasta and cook, stirring occasionally, for 10 to 12 minutes, or until al dente. Pour the pasta into the colander with the peas and drain well; this will defrost the peas and even cook them a bit.

While the pasta is cooking, place the oil in a large skillet over medium-high heat. Add the onion, zucchini, and yellow squash and cook, stirring frequently, for 8 to 10 minutes, or until the vegetables start to get translucent. Add the garlic and cook for 1 minute, then add the tomato, broccoli, and carrot and cook for 2 to 3 minutes, or until the tomatoes are warm. Add the milk and Parmesan cheese to the pan and stir gently for 1 minute. Add the pasta and peas to the pan and stir until combined. Season with salt and pepper, sprinkle with some more Parmesan cheese, and serve immediately.

The National Pasta Association lists fifty-one different types of pasta on their website. With so many to choose from it can be difficult to remember which one works best for what. An easy rule of thumb is that delicate pastas like angel hair should be served with light, thin sauces; thicker pastas such as fettuccine are good for heavier sauces; and pastas with holes, like penne or tube pasta, work well with chunky sauces.

cooking 101

spicy stir-fried greens

J: This dish proves how a few simple ingredients can turn into a wonderful meal. You can add more vegetables if you want, but I say why mess with success? This dish has a hint of spice. If you like things spicier, you can be more generous with the crushed red pepper. **Serves 4**

2¹/4 cups water

1 cup rice

1 head bok choy

1 large onion

1 tablespoon canola oil

1 tablespoon soy sauce

¹/2 teaspoon crushed red pepper

Salt and pepper

¹/2 cup whole almonds or cashews

Almonds are believed to have originated in China and Central Asia and eventually made their way to the Middle East and the Mediterranean. They were used in breads served to Egypt's pharaohs, and ancient Romans showered newlyweds with them as a fertility charm. Knowing that, I think I'll make this dish with cashews.

food trivia

Place the water and rice in a small saucepan and bring to a boil over high heat. Cover and simmer over medium-low heat for 20 minutes, or until most of the water is absorbed. Remove from the heat and let stand for 5 minutes.

Starting at the leafy top of the bok choy, cut it crosswise into ¹/2-inch-thick slices. (As soon as the slices are cut, they'll fall apart into rings, a little like an onion.) Peel the onion, cut it in half, then cut into thin slices.

Heat the oil in a large skillet over medium-high heat. Add the bok choy and onion and cook for 5 minutes. Add the soy sauce and crushed red pepper and cook for 4 to 5 minutes, or until the onion is translucent and the bok choy is tender. Season with salt and pepper.

Spoon some of the rice into the center of each plate, top with the vegetables, and sprinkle with the almonds.

cheesy baked tortellini

j: I made this one day when I was supposed to make dinner for my friends but didn't have much time. They were totally impressed and begged for the recipe. It's really fast to make because it uses premade tortellini. That may seem like a cop-out, but who has time to make tortellini from scratch? Plus, the sauce is super creamy and wonderful! **Serves 4**

1 pound frozen cheese tortellini

8 ounces fresh mushrooms

1 tablespoon canola oil

2 tablespoons butter

1/4 cup flour

2 cups milk

Salt and pepper

1 cup grated Parmesan cheese

Preheat the oven to 400°F.

Bring a large pot of salted water to a boil and add the tortellini. Cook over medium-high heat, stirring occasionally, for 15 minutes, or until cooked through. Drain in a colander and place in a 9-inch baking pan.

Meanwhile, cut the ends off the mushroom stems, discard, and cut the mushrooms into thin slices. Heat the canola oil in a skillet over medium-high heat, add the mushrooms, and cook, stirring frequently, for 12 to 15 minutes, or until the mushrooms are golden brown.

Add the butter to the pan and stir until melted, then stir in the flour and cook for 1 minute. Slowly pour in the milk, stirring continuously. Lower the heat to medium-low and cook for 7 to 8 minutes, or until the sauce just begins to bubble. Remove from the heat, season with salt and pepper, and stir in the Parmesan cheese. Pour the sauce over the tortellini and bake for 20 to 25 minutes, or until the sauce begins to brown. Serve immediately.

Tortellini was first made in the Emilia-Romagna region in northern Italy. Legend has it that Venus, Bacchus, and Mars stopped at an inn one night. The group was so noisy that the innkeeper couldn't resist peeking through the keyhole. He was so inspired by the beauty of Venus's naked body that he shaped a pasta to resemble her perfect navel. You gotta love the Italians—they have the best stories about food.

food trivia

zucchini "casserole"

m : This is called a casserole because when my grandmother makes it she
sautés the vegetables, then puts them in a casserole dish and bakes
them with the cheese on top. You can do that if you want, but I say why
bother? It's faster and easier to cook it all in one pan, and it tastes exactly
the same. As for the breadcrumbs, any kind works, so we usually go with
plain. **Serves 4**

1 onion

4 zucchini

2 tomatoes

2 tablespoons canola oil

1/2 cup breadcrumbs

Salt and pepper

2 cups grated mozzarella or Jack
cheese

Peel and coarsely chop the onion. Remove and discard the
ends of the zucchini. Cut the zucchini in half lengthwise, then
cut into 1/4-inch-thick slices. Cut the tomatoes in half, remove
the seeds by scraping them out of the tomato with a small tool
or your finger, and cut into 1-inch pieces.

Place the canola oil in a large saucepan over medium heat.
Add the onion and zucchini and cook, stirring occasionally, for
12 to 15 minutes, or until the zucchini starts to soften. Add
the tomatoes and cook for 5 minutes. Stir in the breadcrumbs
and season with salt and pepper. Sprinkle the cheese over the
zucchini, cover, and cook without stirring for 5 minutes, or until
the cheese is melted. Serve immediately.

$ **Cheese can be expensive, but there are ways
to lessen the bite. If you're like me and use
a lot of cheese, you can purchase large bags
of grated cheese at a warehouse store, or just
buy a lot when it's on sale at the supermarket.
Either way, store it in your freezer, and just take
out what you need each time. Once the bag is
opened, put the cheese in a heavy (freezer style)
zip-top bag and squeeze all the air out before you
seal it.**

bargain shopper

lentil soup

m : Who doesn't like lentil soup? This soup is as easy as cutting up a few vegetables and putting them in the pot. The hard part—if you're hungry— is waiting for it to cook. This is great on a cold fall day when you need a little something to warm you up. It reheats really well, and you can even freeze it if you have any extra. **Serves 4 to 6**

1 onion

1 carrot

2 stalks celery

2 cloves garlic

1 pound lentils

2 tablespoons canola oil

1 bay leaf

1 teaspoon Italian seasoning

1 (15-ounce) can diced tomatoes

10 cups water

$1/2$ cup frozen chopped spinach or a handful of fresh chopped spinach

Salt and pepper

Peel the onion and carrot and cut into $1/2$-inch pieces. Trim and discard the ends of the celery and dice into $1/2$-inch pieces. Peel and finely chop the garlic or put it through a garlic press. Rinse the lentils in a sieve and pick through them to remove any foreign objects.

Place the oil in a large stockpot over medium heat. Add the onion, carrot, and celery and cook, stirring occasionally, for 10 to 12 minutes, or until the onion is translucent. Stir in the garlic, bay leaf, and Italian seasoning, and cook for 2 minutes. Add the lentils, tomatoes, and water to the pan and bring to a boil. Reduce the heat to low and simmer for 1 hour.

Just prior to serving, stir in the spinach and cook for 2 to 3 minutes, or until warm. Season with salt and pepper and serve immediately.

Don't let directions telling you to remove any foreign objects from lentils freak you out. It's not as scary as it sounds. Because the lentil plants grow close to the ground, it's very common for small stones to get picked up during harvesting. You just need to run your fingers through them as you are rinsing them and take a close look to make sure there aren't any stones.

cooking 101

asian salad

j: This recipe was inspired by an amazing salad I had at an organic restaurant near my house. I love all of the fun stuff in it. The sweetness of the pineapple and the crunch of the chow mein noodles and almonds are a fabulous combination. And the dressing is light, so it doesn't weigh down the salad. It's a perfect hot weather dish. You can get dried pineapple in the bulk food section of a supermarket, or you can usually find them by the other dried fruits. **Serves 4**

1 head Chinese (napa) cabbage

3 green onions

3/4 cup dried pineapple chunks

2 cloves garlic

3 tablespoons canola oil

2 tablespoons rice vinegar

2 tablespoons soy sauce

1 teaspoon peeled, minced fresh ginger

1 1/2 cups dried chow mein noodles

3/4 cup sliced almonds

Rinse the Chinese cabbage, chop it coarsely, and place it in a large bowl. Trim the green onions, discarding the ends, and cut the white and about 1 inch of the green part into thin slices; add them to the cabbage. Cut the dried pineapple into 1/4-inch cubes and add to the cabbage and green onions.

Peel and finely chop the garlic or pass it through a garlic press. Place the oil, vinegar, soy sauce, garlic, and ginger in a small bowl and stir well with a fork.

Add the chow mein noodles and almonds to the bowl with the cabbage, green onions, and pineapple. Pour the dressing over the salad and toss until everything is evenly coated. Serve immediately.

Fresh ginger root can be found in most grocery store produce sections. Be sure to pick ginger that is smooth, un-blemished, and firm. Fresh ginger will keep for a week at room temperature and about a month in the refrig-erator wrapped in plastic wrap. It's a bit hard to peel ginger, so I would suggest using a knife rather than a peeler.

cooking 101

pesto pasta

j: I love all pesto, but when it's homemade you absolutely can't beat it. It's so fresh and delicious that you really don't need to mess with it. This pasta is fabulous hot, but—bonus—it's also great cold. So you can have it for dinner one night and then take the leftovers for lunch the next day. **Serves 4**

1 (²/₃-ounce) package fresh basil

4 cloves garlic

¹/₄ cup grated Parmesan cheese, plus extra for sprinkling

¹/₂ cup olive oil

3 tablespoons pine nuts

2 cups grape tomatoes

1 pound uncooked pasta

Salt and pepper

Remove the stems from the basil and place the leaves in the blender. Peel the garlic and add it to the blender. Add the Parmesan cheese, olive oil, and pine nuts and purée until smooth.

Place the tomatoes in a colander. Bring a large saucepan of salted water to a boil. Add the pasta and cook, stirring occasionally, for 10 minutes, or until al dente. Pour the pasta into the colander over the tomatoes and drain well. Pour the pasta and tomatoes back into the pan and add the pesto. Stir until the pasta is thoroughly coated and season with salt and pepper. Serve immediately.

Pine nuts are the seeds from the pinecones of certain types of pine trees. Unshelled pine nuts have a long shelf life, but once they're shelled they can become rancid within a few weeks. Since they are usually sold shelled in the U.S., make sure you only buy as much as you need and use them promptly. If you end up with more than you need, you can freeze them and take them out when you need them.

cooking 101

cheap eats 2

classic tex-mex tacos

j: Taco seasoning can cover all manner of sins, but when I first saw textured vegetable protein, I was a bit apprehensive: could it possibly taste any better than driveway gravel? As it turns out, it's pretty amazing stuff. In water, it expands to more than twice its original volume, and it picks up the flavors of whatever you combine it with. It has the texture of ground beef, but it's way cheaper. This all makes it perfect for these classic tacos in a crispy shell, which are usually filled with seasoned ground beef. You can buy it at your local produce market or natural foods store in the bulk food section. **Serves 4**

1 onion

2 cloves garlic

1 tablespoon canola oil

1 cup textured vegetable protein

2 cups water

1 (6-ounce) can tomato paste

2 tablespoons Mexican seasoning

12 taco shells

1 cup salsa

2 cups shredded lettuce

1 cup grated Cheddar cheese

Peel the onion and cut it into $1/2$-inch pieces. Peel and finely chop the garlic or pass it through a garlic press. Place the oil in a large skillet, add the onion, and cook for 10 to 12 minutes, or until the onion is translucent. Add the garlic and cook, stirring constantly, for 1 minute. Add the vegetable protein, water, tomato paste, and Mexican seasoning and cook for 10 to 12 minutes, or until all the liquid has been absorbed.

Spoon some of the filling into each taco shell and top with some of the salsa, lettuce, and cheese. Serve them up (don't tell your nonvegetarian friends it's not actually meat—bet they don't guess).

Americans consume about 85 billion tortillas a year (not including tortilla chips). That's a lot of tacos. And burritos. And quesadillas. And enchiladas. Hey—come to think of it I guess I'm doing my part in the great American tortilla binge.

food trivia

baked omelet with onion, spinach, and swiss cheese

J: Eggs are always a good choice when you're on a tight budget. They are loaded with protein, you can make them a million different ways, and they taste great. I think that's the food trifecta. If the idea of making an omelet on the stovetop intimidates you, this one is the perfect solution—just put the pan in the oven, no flipping or folding required. **Serves 4**

Butter or cooking spray

8 eggs

1/2 cup milk

1/2 teaspoon salt

1/4 teaspoon pepper

1/2 small onion

1 cup frozen chopped spinach, thawed and drained (see page 37) or a handful or two of chopped fresh spinach

2 cups grated Swiss cheese

Preheat the oven to 350°F. Lightly coat an 8-inch square baking pan with butter or cooking spray.

Beat the eggs, milk, salt, and pepper in a large bowl until well combined. Peel the onion and cut into 1/4-inch pieces. Spread the onion, spinach, and Swiss cheese evenly in the pan, then pour in the egg mixture. Bake for 45 to 50 minutes, or until a knife inserted into the center comes out clean. Remove from the oven and serve immediately.

Spinach is an excellent source of iron, calcium, chlorophyll, beta-carotene, vitamin C, riboflavin, sodium, and potassium. But keep in mind that fresh spinach loses much of its nutritional value if it's stored more than a few days. Refrigeration slows the effect somewhat, but it is best to use fresh spinach within a couple of days of buying it. Freezing spinach prevents the loss of most of its nutritional value, so frozen spinach is a great choice, too.

food for thought

pasta with broccoli and caramelized onions

m: Of all the dishes in this book, this was probably the favorite when we were testing recipes. Everyone we tried it on loved it. Although it takes a little time to caramelize the onions, it's easy (they pretty much just sit in the pan and cook themselves), and you will not believe how sweet and delicious they end up. **Serves 4**

2 onions

2 tablespoons vegetable oil

1 bunch broccoli

1 pound uncooked salad macaroni or other small pasta

1/4 cup sliced almonds

1 tablespoon balsamic vinegar

Salt and pepper

Peel the onions and cut into thin slices. Place the oil and onion in a large skillet and cook over medium heat for 20 to 25 minutes, or until the onions are golden brown. Remove from the heat and set aside.

While the onions are cooking, cut the florets from the broccoli and discard the stems. Bring a large pot of salted water to a boil and add the pasta. Cook over medium-high heat, stirring occasionally, for 8 minutes, or until al dente. After the pasta has been cooking for 4 minutes, add the broccoli florets to the pasta water for the remainder of the cooking time. Drain the pasta and broccoli in the colander.

Add the drained pasta and broccoli, almonds, and balsamic vinegar to the pan of onions and mix well. Season with salt and pepper and serve immediately.

Balsamic vinegar is made from grapes that have been cooked down to a syrup and then aged. The aging time—anywhere between three and 150 years—is what determines the price. The three-year-old stuff works fine for a college budget (and frankly, we may never in our lives be able to afford the oldest balsamic—it goes for hundreds of dollars an ounce). Cheap but decent balsamic vinegar is nice to have in your pantry—it makes very nice salad dressing when mixed with oil and salt and pepper. Just check the ingredients list to make sure they haven't added caramel or brown sugar to sweeten up an inferior product.

cooking 101

fried rice

j: Fried rice is super easy, yummy, and, shockingly, not necessarily too bad for you. Although our version has the word *fried* in the name, we use cooking spray instead of oil to reduce the calories, and you can also add a little fiber by using brown rice instead of white. See? Actually good for you! Rice is really cheap, and the vegetables in this recipe aren't too expensive either, so this a staple of my diet. **Serves 4**

$2^1/4$ cups water

1 cup white rice

1 bunch green onions

1 cup snow pea pods

2 cloves garlic

Cooking spray

2 eggs

2 cups bean sprouts

$1/2$ cup frozen peas

$1/4$ cup soy sauce

Place the water and rice in a small saucepan and bring to a boil over high heat. Cover and simmer over medium-low heat for 20 minutes, or until most of the water has been absorbed. Remove from the heat and let stand for 5 minutes.

Trim the green onions, discarding the ends, and cut the white and about 1 inch of the green part into thin slices. Cut the snow pea pods into thirds. Peel and finely chop the garlic or pass it through a garlic press.

Coat a large skillet with cooking spray and place over medium heat. Beat the eggs slightly and pour into the pan. Cook, stirring frequently, for 2 to 3 minutes, or until scrambled. Remove the eggs from the pan and set them aside.

Remove the pan from the heat and wipe out the pan with wadded-up paper towels. Recoat with cooking spray, and place over medium-high heat. Add the snow peas and bean sprouts to the pan. Cook, stirring frequently, for 3 to 4 minutes, or until the bean sprouts just begin to wilt. Add the green onions, garlic, and frozen peas to the pan and cook, stirring frequently, for 2 minutes. Stir in the cooked rice, eggs, and soy sauce and cook for 3 to 4 minutes, or until heated through. Serve immediately.

Fried rice is one of the original thrifty leftover dishes. Leftover cooked rice gets a little dried out in the fridge, so it's not too pleasant to reheat and eat. But when you cook it up with some eggs and veggies, it gets a whole new life. And fried rice makes a good leftover itself: even if you're just making it for yourself, make the whole batch and refrigerate the rest to eat later or take with you for lunch.

cooking 101

spicy potato samosas

m : If you like curry and crispy fried foods, you'll love these Indian-style turnovers. The filling can be prepared in advance and kept in the fridge until
you're ready to eat. We use wonton wrappers for the dough, so all you
have to do is fill them and fry them when you're ready. **Serves 4**

1 small onion

2 cloves garlic

2 large potatoes (about
1 1/2 pounds)

2 jalapeño peppers

Canola oil

1 teaspoon minced fresh ginger

1/2 cup frozen peas

2 teaspoons curry powder

1 teaspoon salt

2 tablespoons chopped cilantro

2 teaspoons lemon juice

12 (6-inch) wonton wrappers

Peel the onion and cut into 1/4-inch pieces. Peel and finely
chop the garlic or pass it through a garlic press. Peel the potatoes and cut into 1/4-inch pieces. Cut the jalapeños in half,
remove the seeds, and finely chop.

Place 2 tablespoons of the oil in a large nonstick skillet over
medium-high heat. Add the onion, garlic, and potatoes and
cook, stirring frequently, for 10 to 12 minutes. Add the jalapeños, ginger, and peas and cook, stirring frequently, for 5 to
7 minutes, or until the potatoes are cooked. Add the curry
powder, salt, cilantro, and lemon juice and cook for 2 minutes.

Spoon about 1/4 cup of filling into the center of each wonton
wrapper. Wet your finger with water, dampen the entire edge
of the wrapper, and fold the wrapper over the filling. Press the
edges together to seal. Repeat until all the wrappers are filled.

Heat about 2 inches of canola oil in a large saucepan until very
hot (depending on the size of your pan, you'll need about 2 to
3 cups). Add 2 samosas to the pan at a time and cook for 5 to
7 minutes on each side, or until golden brown. Remove with a
slotted spoon and drain on paper towels. Serve immediately.

**Curry is an Indian blend of up to twenty
spices and seeds. The chief ingredient is
usually turmeric, which provides its characteristic
yellowish color. Other common ingredients include
black pepper, cardamom, chiles, cinnamon, cloves,
coriander, cumin, fennel seed, fenugreek, ginger,
mace, nutmeg, pimiento, poppy seeds, red pepper,
saffron, sesame seeds, and tamarind. You can buy
curry powder in the supermarket; just be aware
that if the jar has been around for more than
6 months it will have lost a lot of its punch, so you
may want to use a bit more.**

cooking 101

potato and sweet potato tart

j: This is so easy to make, and it's a tasty, cheap comfort food dish. It's a little bit like an open-face pot pie, and the combo of roasted sweet potato and pastry, with a little hit of nutmeg, tips it just a tiny bit in the direction of dessert. This cannot be a bad thing. This will feed four for dinner, or eight if you are serving it as an appetizer. **Serves 4**

1 prepared piecrust (see page 5)

2 potatoes

1 sweet potato

2 tablespoons flour

2 tablespoons melted butter

$1/2$ cup milk

Salt and pepper

$1/2$ teaspoon ground nutmeg

Preheat the oven to 350°F. Press the piecrust gently into an ungreased 9-inch tart pan or deep dish pie pan.

Peel the potatoes and sweet potato and cut them into thin, even slices (no more than $1/8$ inch thick). Combine the flour and melted butter and slowly add the milk, stirring until smooth; there should be no lumps. Place a single layer of potato slices in the bottom of the tart pan, spread 2 tablespoons of the milk mixture over the potatoes, and season with salt and pepper. Place a layer of sweet potatoes over the potatoes, spread with 2 tablespoons of the milk mixture, and season with salt and pepper. Continue layering until you have 3 layers of white potatoes and 2 of sweet potatoes. Sprinkle with the nutmeg and bake for 45 to 50 minutes, or until the top layer and the crust are lightly browned. Serve immediately.

Nutmeg is a seed growing on an evergreen tree in the Spice Islands of Indonesia. It's not as coveted as it used to be in, say, the fifteenth century, when Columbus sailed west looking for it, but it's still an essential ingredient in eggnog and pumpkin pie. It's poisonous in large quantities, but not to worry—you'd have to down A LOT of it to make yourself sick.

food trivia

orzo salad

m : We use dried herbs as much as possible because it's easier to have them on hand and they're cheaper. But this is one of the cases where dried herbs just won't work. Not that the other ingredients in this salad aren't good, but the fresh tarragon, which has a light licorice flavor, makes this dish what it is. Don't even bother making it with dried tarragon. **Serves 4**

1 1/2 cups uncooked orzo

1/2 red bell pepper

1 cup grape tomatoes

1/4 cup finely chopped red onion

2 tablespoons chopped fresh tarragon

1/4 cup lemon juice

3 tablespoons olive oil

Salt and pepper

1/2 cup crumbled feta cheese

Bring a large saucepan of salted water to a boil. Add the orzo and cook for 8 minutes, or until al dente. Drain in a sieve and run under cold water to chill, then transfer to a large serving bowl.

Cut the bell pepper in half lengthwise and remove the stem, seeds, and pale membranes. Cut the pepper flesh into squarish 1/4-inch pieces. Add the bell pepper to the orzo, along with the tomatoes, onion, and tarragon, and stir until combined.

Place the lemon juice and olive in a small bowl and whisk with a fork until combined. Pour the dressing over the pasta and vegetables and stir well. Season with salt and pepper and serve topped with the feta cheese.

? Although orzo is small and rice shaped, it is actually a pasta made from semolina, which is the most common pasta grain. Like a lot of pasta names, orzo (which is Italian for "barley") describes the shape of the pasta in a metaphorical way: for example, lumache ("snails"), spaghetti ("little strings"), or agnolotti ("priests' caps").

food trivia

crispy polenta with sautéed vegetables

m : This recipe is a spin on something I tasted in France, and I don't mind saying that we've done a way better job than they did. Cooking the polenta from scratch gives the best results, but you could also buy a roll of cooked polenta (find it near the pasta in the supermarket). Trim a little off the ends of the roll and slice it into eight slices. Brown two slices for each serving. **Serves 4**

2 cups water

1 vegetable bouillon cube

2 tablespoons butter

1 cup uncooked polenta

1 clove garlic

1 red onion

1 zucchini

1 yellow squash

1 red bell pepper

3 tablespoons canola oil

Salt and pepper

2 tablespoons balsamic vinegar

$ **Polenta is a slightly coarser grind of corn than cornmeal, yet because of its gourmet connotations, it's much more expensive. Using cornmeal instead of polenta in this recipe won't make any difference in the taste, but it will make a difference in your wallet.**

bargain shopper

Line an 8- or 9-inch baking pan with plastic wrap.

Bring the water, bouillon cube, and butter to a boil in a saucepan. Slowly pour the polenta into the pan, stirring constantly. Lower the heat to medium-low and cook, stirring frequently, for 20 to 25 minutes, or until creamy. Spread the polenta evenly in the prepared pan and refrigerate until completely cooled, about 30 minutes.

While the polenta is cooling, peel and finely chop the garlic or pass it through a garlic press. Peel the onion, cut it in half, then cut into 1/4-inch-thick slices. Cut the zucchini and yellow squash into 1/4-inch-thick slices. Cut the bell pepper in half, remove the seeds and membranes, and cut into thin slices.

Heat 2 tablespoons of the oil in a large skillet and add the garlic, onion, zucchini, yellow squash, and bell pepper. Cook, stirring frequently, for 15 to 20 minutes, or until the vegetables are tender. Season with salt and pepper and stir in the balsamic vinegar. Remove the vegetables from the pan to a bowl and set aside. Wipe the pan clean with a paper towel and return it to the stovetop.

Cut the cooled polenta into 4 squares, then cut each square into 2 triangles. Heat the remaining 1 tablespoon of oil in the pan over medium-high heat and add the polenta triangles. Cook for 4 to 5 minutes, or until lightly browned, then flip the squares over and cook for 4 to 5 minutes on the other side.

Place 2 pieces of crispy polenta on each of 4 plates and top with some of the vegetables. Serve immediately.

spinach-mushroom crêpes

j: Crêpes are incredibly delicious and probably one of the most versatile foods you can make. They feel fancy and sound impressive, but are fairly cheap to make. When you make these, do not, I repeat do not use the so-called Parmesan that comes in a green shaker can. Use the real stuff; you'll need about 3 ounces to make 1 cup. **Serves 4**

4 eggs

1 1/3 cups milk

2 tablespoons vegetable oil, plus extra for wiping pan

1 cup flour

1 small onion

8 ounces mushrooms

2 tablespoons butter

1 pound frozen chopped spinach, thawed and drained (see Cooking 101, below), or 2 pounds fresh spinach

1 cup grated Parmesan cheese

1/2 cup sour cream

Salt and pepper

To thaw frozen spinach, let the spinach sit at room temperature for about 30 minutes, or until thawed. (Alternatively, if you have a microwave, place the spinach in a microwave-safe bowl and cook on high heat for 3 minutes, or until thawed.) Drain the spinach in a strainer, pressing it with the back of a spoon to remove any excess water.

cooking 101

Crack the eggs into a blender and pulse a few times to beat them a bit. Add the milk, oil, and flour and blend until smooth.

Heat an 8-inch nonstick skillet over medium heat. Place a small amount of oil on a paper towel and rub it over the surface of the pan. (You only need a tiny bit of oil; if you use more, the crêpes take much longer to cook and get greasy.) Pour in 1/4 cup of the crêpe batter and quickly swirl and tip the pan, rolling the batter around until it covers the entire bottom of the pan. Cook for 2 minutes, or until the crêpe is set in the center. With a rubber spatula, loosen the edges of the crêpe and flip it over. Cook for 1 minute, then remove from the pan. Repeat the process with the remaining batter, oiling the pan before making each crêpe. Stack the cooked crêpes on top of each other and gently pull them apart when you're ready to use them, or stack them separated by pieces of wax paper to keep them from sticking together.

Peel the onion and cut into 1/4-inch pieces. Cut the ends off the mushroom stems, discard, and cut the mushrooms into thin slices. Place the butter in a large skillet over medium-high heat. Add the onion and mushrooms and cook, stirring frequently, for 10 to 12 minutes, or until the onions are translucent and the mushrooms are soft. Add the spinach and cook, stirring frequently, for 5 minutes, or until the mixture is hot and most of the liquid has evaporated. Add the Parmesan and sour cream and cook, stirring occasionally, for 2 to 3 minutes, or until the filling is warm and well combined. Season with salt and pepper.

Place a crêpe in the center of each plate. Spoon about 1/3 cup of the spinach mixture down the center of each crêpe and fold in the sides to form a roll. Gently roll the crêpe over so the seam side is down, then continue filling and folding the crêpes until there are 3 rolled crêpes on each plate. Spoon any extra spinach mixture over the crêpes and serve immediately.

penne with pan-roasted tomatoes and white beans

j: This pasta dish is pretty spectacular. It's just a few ingredients that combine to make something fabulous—and that, in a nutshell, is the secret of Italian cooking. The roasted tomatoes and roasted garlic are rich and delicious, the beans add protein and texture, and the basil brings a fresh flavor. **Serves 4**

1 pound uncooked penne pasta

4 Roma tomatoes

3 cloves garlic

1/4 cup fresh basil leaves

1 tablespoon olive oil

1 (15-ounce) can white beans

Salt and pepper

1/4 cup grated Parmesan cheese

Bring a large pot of salted water to a boil. Add the pasta and cook over medium-high heat, stirring occasionally, for 10 minutes, or until al dente. Drain the pasta in a colander and return it to the pot.

Meanwhile, cut the tomatoes in half, scrape the seeds out of each half with a small tool or your finger, and cut into 1-inch pieces. Peel the garlic and leave the cloves whole. Coarsely chop the basil leaves.

Heat the oil in a large skillet over medium heat. Add the tomatoes and garlic, cover, and cook for 10 to 12 minutes, or until the garlic is soft. Remove the garlic from the pan and set aside. Put the beans in a strainer and rinse under running water. Drain the beans and add them to the pan, then remove the pan from the heat. Smash the garlic with a fork and add it to the drained pasta. Add the tomatoes and basil, stir well, and season with salt and pepper. Pour the pasta into a large serving bowl, sprinkle with the Parmesan cheese, and serve immediately.

> **Basil is native to India, though it's since become integral to the cooking of countries as far afield as Italy and Thailand. When it migrated to Italy, it became a symbol of love, with young women wearing sprigs in their hair to encourage their suitors.**
>
> **food trivia**

falafel pita with cucumber sauce

m: Make this for your friends. They won't believe that it didn't come from that little Mediterranean place around the corner. This is a great recipe to partially prepare in advance and refrigerate until you're ready to cook and eat, but once you cook the falafel, it's best to eat it right away. This sauce is good on anything from veggies to bread. I like to make extra just for snacking on. **Serves 4**

1 (15-ounce) can chickpeas

1 onion

5 cloves garlic

2 tablespoons finely chopped fresh parsley

1 teaspoon ground cumin

2 tablespoons flour

Salt and pepper

Canola oil for frying

1 cup sour cream

$^1/_2$ cucumber

1 carrot

1 tomato

2 pieces pita bread

Temperature control is the key to nongreasy frying: if your oil is hot enough when you add the food, and if it stays hot enough, the food will cook fast and absorb a surprisingly small amount of oil. Fry the food in batches to keep the pan uncrowded— adding a lot of food to the pan can cool the oil down too much.

cooking 101

Pour the chickpeas into a colander and rinse under cold water. Let drain for 10 minutes. Place the chickpeas in a bowl and smash them well with a fork or a potato masher, if you have one, until they are the consistency of dense, grainy mashed potatoes. Peel and finely chop the onion and garlic, or pass the garlic through a garlic press. Reserve 1 tablespoon of the chopped onion and 1 teaspoon of the chopped garlic for the sauce and add the remainder of each to the mashed chickpeas. Stir in the parsley, cumin, and flour until they are completely combined. Season with salt and pepper and mix well. Form the mixture into small balls about the size of ping-pong balls, and press them gently between your palms to flatten slightly into patties.

Pour about 1 inch of oil into a deep skillet or large saucepan and place over medium-high heat until very hot (about 350°F). (A tiny drop of water flicked into the pan should immediately cause the oil to bubble up.) Carefully add a few of the patties to the oil using a slotted spoon. Make sure not to crowd the patties in the pan. Cook for 3 to 4 minutes on each side, or until golden brown. Remove to a plate lined with several layers of paper towels to drain and repeat the process with the remaining patties.

Place the sour cream in a bowl and add the reserved onion and garlic. Peel the cucumber and cut it in half lengthwise. Scrape out the seeds with a spoon and cut the cucumber into thin slices. Stir the cucumber into the sour cream and season with salt and pepper.

Peel and grate the carrot. Cut the tomato in half, remove the seeds by scraping them out of the tomato with a small tool or your finger, and chop into $^1/_2$-inch pieces. Cut the pita breads in half and open the pockets. Place 3 or 4 falafel in each pocket and spoon on some of the cucumber sauce. Top with some of the grated carrot and tomato and serve immediately.

avoiding the freshman fifteen 3

lettuce wraps

These are light and healthy, and so packed with flavor that everyone will love them. The sauce has a classic combo of Southeast Asian flavors that go so well together—salty, sweet, sour, and spicy. Just be careful with the chili paste. It's hot . . . really hot. **Serves 4 to 6**

Sauce

$1/2$ cup soy sauce

$2/3$ cup lime juice

2 tablespoons brown sugar

1 tablespoon chili paste

Wraps

1 onion

2 cloves garlic

2 small zucchini

1 pound mushrooms

1 (8-ounce) can bamboo shoots

1 cucumber

$1/2$ red bell pepper

1 head iceberg or butter lettuce

1 tablespoon finely chopped ginger

Cooking spray

$1/2$ cup chopped salted peanuts

Chili paste is a blend of hot chile peppers, garlic, and oil and is used in many different Asian dishes. You can find it by the Asian foods in most grocery stores. If you've never used it before, start with a little and add more to suit your tastes.

cooking 101

To prepare the sauce: Place the soy sauce, lime juice, brown sugar, and chili paste in a small bowl and stir until combined.

To prepare the wraps: Peel the onion and cut into $1/4$-inch pieces. Peel and finely chop the garlic or pass it through a garlic press. Trim the zucchini and mushroom stems, discarding the ends, and dice into $1/4$-inch pieces. Drain the bamboo shoots and cut into $1/4$-inch pieces. Peel the cucumber, cut into matchstick-sized pieces (about $1/8$ by $1/8$ by 2 inches), and set aside (you'll use these for garnish). Halve the bell pepper, remove and discard the stem, seeds, and pale membranes, cut the pepper flesh into very thin slices, and set aside (more garnish). Separate the lettuce leaves from the head, wash, and let dry on paper towels. Place the lettuce, cucumber, and bell pepper on a plate, cover with plastic wrap, and refrigerate until ready to serve.

Coat a large skillet with cooking spray and add the onion. Cook over medium heat, stirring occasionally, for 10 to 12 minutes, or until the onion is translucent. Add the garlic, zucchini, and mushrooms, cover, and cook over medium-high heat, stirring occasionally, for 5 minutes. Add the bamboo shoots, ginger, and half of the sauce and cook, uncovered, for 2 to 3 minutes, or until most of the liquid has been absorbed.

Place the filling in a bowl and serve with the lettuce leaves, cucumber, bell pepper, peanuts, and remaining sauce on the side. To assemble, place some of the filling inside a lettuce leaf. Arrange some of the cucumber and bell pepper over the filling. Sprinkle with some of the chopped peanuts, drizzle with the sauce, and wrap up like a burrito.

teriyaki tofu with vegetables

j: I love teriyaki sauce. For me, anything can be made better with teriyaki sauce, which is why I was totally in favor of the tofu in this recipe, much to my sister's surprise. The tofu soaks up a light teriyaki flavor, but not so much that it becomes overly teriyaki-y. I made that up, but it should be a word. **Serves 4**

1 (8-ounce) package baked tofu, any flavor

$1/2$ cup teriyaki sauce

1 small head bok choy

2 stalks celery

1 carrot

1 small onion

2 cloves garlic

Cooking spray

1 (8-ounce) can sliced water chestnuts

1 tablespoon cornstarch

2 cups cooked white rice (see page 6)

Cut the tofu into bite-size pieces, place in a shallow bowl, and pour in the teriyaki sauce. Let stand, stirring occasionally, until ready to use.

Rinse the bok choy and cut both leaves and stems into $1/4$-inch-thick slices. Trim and discard the ends of the celery and cut it into $1/4$-inch-thick slices. Peel the carrot and onion and cut into thin slices. Peel and finely chop the garlic or pass it through a garlic press.

Generously spray a large skillet with cooking spray and place over medium-high heat. Add the garlic to the pan and cook, stirring constantly, for 30 seconds. Add the bok choy, celery, carrot, onion, and water chestnuts and cook, stirring frequently, for 4 to 5 minutes, or until the carrot is just tender. Add the tofu to the pan, reserving the teriyaki sauce. Combine the cornstarch and teriyaki sauce, stir until smooth, then stir in to the pan. Cook, stirring constantly, for 2 to 3 minutes, or until the sauce comes to a boil. Take the pan off the heat.

Spoon some of the rice onto each plate, top with some of the tofu mixture, and serve immediately.

> **You may have heard that eating celery burns more calories than it contains, making it a "negative calorie" food. Although that is technically correct, don't get your hopes up that you are going to eat your way thin. The negative calories are due more to the fact that there are so few calories in celery than that you burn off so many eating it.**
>
> **food trivia**

eggplant curry

m : I never realized that there were so many ways to make curry until a few of my friends got into a discussion of the virtues of the different types. There's red, made with red chiles; green, made with green chiles; and yellow, made with turmeric. Countries all across Asia, from India to Malaysia to Thailand (and Mongolia!), have dishes called curries—all spicy. Then there's the wet/dry divide, which has to do with how much sauce the dish has. In case you're interested, this is a dry, yellow, Indian-style curry. **Serves 4**

4 green onions

1 large eggplant

2 potatoes

1 large onion

1 red bell pepper

3 cloves garlic

2 tablespoons olive oil

1 (15-ounce) can diced tomatoes

3 tablespoons curry powder

1 cup water

1/2 vegetable bouillon cube

Salt and pepper

2 cups cooked jasmine rice (see page 6)

Trim the green onions, discarding the ends, and cut the white and about 1 inch of the green part into thin slices. Trim and discard the stem of the eggplant, then peel it and cut into 1-inch cubes. Peel the potatoes and cut into 3/4-inch cubes. Peel the onion and cut into 1/2-inch pieces. Cut the bell pepper in half, remove the stem, seeds, and membranes, and cut into 1/3-inch pieces. Peel and finely chop the garlic or pass it through a garlic press.

Heat the oil in a large skillet over medium-high heat. Add the eggplant, potato, onion, and bell pepper, cover, and cook, stirring occasionally, for 10 to 12 minutes. Add the garlic and cook, uncovered, for 1 minute. Drain the tomatoes and add to the pan along with the curry powder, the water, and the bouillon cube. Simmer over low heat for 5 to 7 minutes, or until the potatoes are tender, then season with salt and pepper.

Spoon the rice into 4 shallow bowls and top with the curry. Sprinkle with the green onions and serve immediately.

Eggplant is probably one of the least appreciated vegetables in the Western world. As a cousin to belladonna, or deadly nightshade, Europeans believed it induced insanity and called it the "mad apple" until just two hundred years ago. Fortunately, Asians didn't share those beliefs. They began cultivating eggplant (which is native to India) as early as the fifth century B.C.E.

food trivia

tempeh stir-fry

m: Here's another easy and fast stir-fry dish that incorporates tempeh, which is a great meat substitute. Served over rice, this is a perfect dish to eat on a day you work out or are extra busy and need some long-lasting energy—it's got good lean protein. **Serves 4**

1 (8-ounce) package tempeh

1 onion

2 cloves garlic

1 cup water

1/4 cup soy sauce

1 tablespoon cornstarch

4 cups broccoli florets

1 tablespoon canola oil

2 cups bean sprouts

2 cups cooked white or brown rice (see page 6)

Cut the tempeh into bite-size pieces. Peel the onion and cut into thin slices. Peel and finely chop the garlic or pass it through a garlic press. Combine the water, soy sauce, and cornstarch in a small bowl, stir until smooth, and set aside.

Place a large saucepan with 1 inch of water over high heat and bring to a boil. Add the broccoli to the pan, cover, and cook for 4 to 5 minutes, or until tender. Drain the water and set aside. (Alternatively, if you have a microwave, place the broccoli in a microwave-safe container and add a little water. Cover with plastic wrap or wax paper and microwave on high heat for 4 to 5 minutes, or until tender.)

Heat the oil in a large skillet over medium-high heat. Add the onion and cook, stirring frequently, for 10 minutes, or until the onion is translucent. Add the garlic, bean sprouts, and tempeh and cook, stirring frequently, for 2 to 3 minutes, or until the bean sprouts just start to soften. Add the soy sauce mixture to the pan and cook, stirring constantly, for 2 to 3 minutes, or until the sauce begins to boil. Remove from the heat and stir in the broccoli.

Spoon some of the rice into the center of each plate and top with the stir-fry.

Tempeh (pronounced "TEM-pay") has been a traditional food and a staple source of protein in Indonesia for several hundred years. It is made by a fermentation process that binds soybeans (and sometimes other beans or grains) together into a cake. It has a tender, chewy consistency but holds together well, making it a good choice for grilling or stir-frying.

cooking 101

spaghetti squash with spicy tomato sauce

j: For me, spaghetti sauce usually means a jar of whatever is on sale at the grocery store, so I wasn't sure about how a spicy spaghetti sauce of my own creation would turn out. I have a tendency to forget that a little bit of spice goes a long way and end up sweating my way through meals. But this time I kept it under control and came up with something that isn't particularly spicy at first but has a bit of a kick at the end. Spaghetti squash is the perfect way to keep calories in check. It has a taste and texture similar to pasta, but only about one-quarter of the calories. **Serves 4**

1 large spaghetti squash (3^1/$_2$ to 4 pounds)

1 large onion

4 cloves garlic

1 tablespoon olive oil

1 teaspoon Italian seasoning

^{1}/$_2$ teaspoon crushed red pepper

1 (6-ounce) can tomato paste

1 (14-ounce) can diced tomatoes

^{3}/$_4$ cup water

1 tablespoon sugar

Salt and pepper

Preheat the oven to 350°F.

Cut the spaghetti squash in half and remove the seeds and soft strings with a large spoon. Place the squash cut side down in a baking pan and bake for 1 hour, or until a fork easily slides into the squash.

While the squash is in the oven, peel the onion and cut into ^{1}/$_4$-inch pieces. Peel and finely chop the garlic or pass it through a garlic press. Place the olive oil in a saucepan over medium heat. Add the onion and cook, stirring occasionally, for 10 to 12 minutes, or until lightly browned. Add the garlic, Italian seasoning, and crushed red pepper and cook, stirring constantly, for 1 minute. Add the tomato paste, tomatoes with their juice, water, and sugar and simmer over low heat for 30 minutes. Season with salt and pepper.

When the squash is cooked, take it out of the oven and, holding each of the squash halves with a hot pad, scrape the insides with a fork to remove and separate the squash strands. Place some of the spaghetti squash "noodles" on each of 4 plates and top with the sauce.

Although spaghetti squash is considered a winter squash, it's available year-round. When buying it, look for smooth, firm squash without ridges, bumps, or spots. It can be stored for several weeks at room temperature and even longer refrigerated. On top of all that, 1 cup of spaghetti squash contains only 45 calories, is an excellent source of folic acid, and is high in fiber. What more could you ask for?

cooking 101

vegetable barley soup

J: Soup is great because you can make a lot when you have time and freeze it in smaller portions so that you always have a quick home-cooked meal on hand. You can even take the frozen soup with you if you have access to a microwave to reheat it. Plus, it is chock-full of vegetables and pretty low in calories.
Serves 4 to 6

2 stalks celery

2 carrots

2 potatoes

4 vegetable bouillon cubes

8 cups water

1 cup pearl barley

8 ounces fresh green beans

1 (15-ounce) can corn kernels

Salt and pepper

Trim and discard the ends of the celery, cut into 1/4-inch-thick slices, and place in a large saucepan. Peel the carrots, cut into 1/4-inch-thick slices, and add to the saucepan. Peel the potatoes, cut into 1/2-inch cubes, and add to the pan. Add the bouillon cubes and water to the pan and bring to a boil. Stir in the barley and cook over medium heat for 30 minutes.

Meanwhile, trim and discard the ends of the green beans and cut into 1-inch pieces. Add the green beans and the corn with its liquid to the pan and cook for 10 to 12 minutes, or until the beans are tender. Season with salt and pepper and serve.

Barley may have been cultivated longer than any other grain in the world—though rice is another contender for this distinction. Barley is similar to pasta in calories, protein, vitamin, and mineral content; however, it is three times as high in dietary fiber. It has also been shown to lower cholesterol levels.

food for thought

asparagus quinoa salad

m: Quin-what?! Okay, so maybe you haven't ever heard of quinoa (pronounced "KEEN-wa"), but this "wonder grain" (actually a seed) is deliciously nutty and chewy and exceptionally nutritious. This salad makes a great meal, and you can take any leftovers for lunch. What I like the best is that it's a nice alternative to the standard pasta salad. **Serves 4 to 6**

1 cup quinoa

2 cups water

Salt

12 spears asparagus

$^1\!/_2$ cup pitted kalamata olives

1 large tomato

1 lemon

1 tablespoon olive oil

Pepper

4 ounces crumbled feta cheese

$ Grains such as quinoa, bulgur wheat, and rice are available prepackaged in most grocery stores. But you can save a substantial amount of money by purchasing them from the bulk food section at a natural food store. For that matter, many supermarkets now have bulk food sections, too.

bargain shopper

Put the quinoa in a strainer and rinse it for a minute or two under running water. Put the water and a pinch of salt in a medium saucepan over high heat and bring to a boil. Stir in the quinoa, lower the heat to medium-low, cover, and cook over medium-low heat for 20 minutes, or until soft. (When it's done, the quinoa seeds will have little wisps spiraling off of them—this is the germ separating from the seed.) Drain the quinoa in a strainer.

While the quinoa is cooking, break off and discard the tough ends of the asparagus and cut the asparagus into 1-inch pieces. Place in a saucepan, add about $^1\!/_2$ inch of water, and bring to a boil. Cover and cook over medium-low heat for 3 to 4 minutes, or until barely tender. (Alternatively, if you have a microwave, place the asparagus in a microwave-safe bowl. Add a few tablespoons of water, cover with plastic wrap or wax paper, and microwave on high heat for 3 to 4 minutes, or until barely tender.) Drain the asparagus and place it under cold running water for 1 minute to cool it down.

Cut the kalamata olives into thin slices. Cut the tomato in half, scrape the seeds out of the tomato with a small tool or your finger, and chop into $^1\!/_2$-inch pieces. Finely grate 1 teaspoon of the lemon peel. Be careful to only grate the yellow part; the white pith underneath is bitter. Squeeze 3 tablespoons of juice from the lemon.

Place the quinoa in a bowl with the asparagus, kalamata olives, tomato, and lemon zest and stir until combined. Whisk together the lemon juice and olive oil and pour over the quinoa mixture. Stir well and season with salt and pepper. Serve topped with the feta cheese.

pasta with braised leeks and winter squash

m : So, I know pasta and winter squash sounds like a strange combination, but I promise it's really good. Not only that, but all the colors make this a beautiful dish as well. The easiest way to peel the squash is to cut it into quarters first, then scrape out the seeds and cut off the peel. Because they're so hard, if I do it any other way I'm afraid my knife will slip and I'll cut myself. **Serves 4**

2 large leeks

1 butternut squash (about 2 pounds)

3 cloves garlic, minced

$1/2$ teaspoon crushed red pepper

$1^1/2$ cups water

1 vegetable bouillon cube

12 ounces uncooked pasta

Salt and pepper

$3/4$ cup grated Parmesan cheese

Remove and discard the root end and the dark green leaves of the leeks, cut the remaining white and light green parts of the leeks in half lengthwise, and rinse the leeks well under running water—really get in there: dirt tends to lurk among the leek's inner layers. Cut the leek halves crosswise into $1/2$-inch-thick slices. Cut the squash in half across the neck, then put the halves cut side down on the cutting board and cut each half in half. Scoop out the seeds and strings with a spoon. Peel the squash with a vegetable peeler or cut it off with your knife, and cut into $3/4$-inch chunks. Peel and finely chop the garlic or pass it through the garlic press.

Place the squash, leeks, garlic, crushed red pepper, water, and bouillon cube in a large saucepan. Bring to a boil and cook over medium heat, stirring occasionally, for 12 to 15 minutes, or until the squash is tender.

Meanwhile, bring a large pot of salted water to a boil over medium-high heat and add the pasta. Cook, stirring occasionally, for 10 minutes, or until al dente. Drain the pasta in a colander. Season the sauce with salt and pepper, then stir in the Parmesan cheese and pasta. Serve immediately.

Consider switching to whole wheat or multi-grain pasta. It really doesn't taste much different, and it's much higher in fiber. But here's a tip from experience: don't cook it as long as the package says. Whole-grain pasta can get mushy when overcooked.

food for thought

green bean salad

m: This is a great dish for a hot summer day when you need something light. The fresh green beans and grape tomatoes make for a delicious salad that's nice for picnics, or to take along on a day when you don't have time to stop at home for lunch. **Serves 4**

2 pounds fresh green beans

1/2 small red onion

2 cloves garlic

1 cup grape tomatoes

1/4 cup cider vinegar

2 teaspoons sugar

1 tablespoon canola oil

Salt and pepper

Cut off and discard the ends of the beans and cut into 1 1/2-inch pieces. Peel and finely chop the onion and garlic or pass the garlic through a garlic press.

Bring a large pot of salted water to a boil. Add the beans and cook for 10 to 12 minutes, or until barely tender. Drain in a colander and rinse with cold water to stop the cooking. Place the beans, onion, garlic, and tomatoes in a bowl.

Place the cider vinegar and sugar in a small bowl. Whisk in the oil with a fork until well combined, then pour over the beans. Season with salt and pepper and refrigerate until ready to serve.

Green beans are loaded with vitamins A, K, and C, manganese, potassium, fiber, folate, iron, omega-3 fatty acids, niacin, and too many more good things to name. The bottom line is, your mother was right. You should eat your green beans.

food for thought

fettuccine with asparagus and lemon

m: This recipe is one of my personal favorites. Using milk instead of cream and cutting down on the Parmesan cheese makes a waistline-friendly alternative to alfredo sauce. I love lemon in just about anything, and together with the asparagus it makes for a light and refreshing pasta dish. The best part is how easy it is. You can do all of the other preparation in the time it takes to cook the pasta. **Serves 4**

12 ounces uncooked fettuccine

1 pound asparagus

1 lemon

1 egg

1 cup milk

2 tablespoons grated Parmesan cheese

Salt and pepper

Bring a large pot of salted water to a boil and add the fettuccine. Cook over medium-high heat, stirring occasionally, for 12 minutes, or until al dente. Drain the fettuccine in a colander.

Meanwhile, break the tough ends off the asparagus, discard, and cut the asparagus into 1-inch pieces. Place in a saucepan, add about 1/2 inch of water, and bring to a boil. Cover and cook over medium-low heat for 3 to 4 minutes, or until barely tender. (Alternatively, if you have a microwave, place the asparagus in a microwave-safe bowl. Add a few tablespoons of water, cover with plastic wrap or wax paper, and microwave on high heat for 3 to 4 minutes, or until barely tender.)

Finely grate 1 tablespoon of the lemon peel. Be careful to only grate the yellow part; the white pith underneath is bitter. Squeeze 2 tablespoons of juice from the lemon.

Whisk together the egg and milk in a large saucepan. Cook over medium heat for 4 to 5 minutes, or until very warm. Don't let it boil, or it will curdle. Remove from the heat, add the Parmesan cheese, asparagus, lemon zest, and lemon juice, and stir until combined. Add the fettuccine and toss until completely coated. Season with salt and pepper and serve immediately.

> **When buying asparagus, look for firm spears with closed tips that are uniform in size, so all of the spears cook in the same amount of time. And contrary to popular belief, spears with a larger diameter are actually more tender than smaller ones.**
>
> **cooking 101**

tabouleh

m: Okay, I like tabouleh, but obviously not as much as the people in a town in the Metn district of Lebanon. They are listed in the Guinness World Records for making the world's largest bowl of tabouleh. It weighed in at a hefty 1,514 kilograms. That's 3,338 pounds of tabouleh. Where do you suppose they got a bowl that big? **Serves 4**

2 cups water

1/2 teaspoon salt

3/4 cup bulgur

1/2 bunch parsley

1 cucumber

2 tomatoes

3 green onions

1 clove garlic

1/4 cup lemon juice

2 tablespoons olive oil

Salt and pepper

1/4 cup coarsely chopped mint leaves

Bring the water and salt to a boil in a saucepan, pour in the bulgur, and cover. Remove from the heat and let stand for 20 minutes, or until most of the liquid has been absorbed and the bulgur is fluffy and tender. Drain in a sieve and refrigerate until ready to use.

Coarsely chop the parsley. Peel the cucumber and cut into 1/2-inch cubes. Cut the tomatoes in half, scrape the seeds out of the tomato with a small tool or your finger, and cut into 1/2-inch pieces. Trim the green onions, discarding the ends, and cut the white and about 1 inch of the green part into thin slices.

Peel and finely chop the garlic or pass it through a garlic press, place it in a small bowl with the lemon juice and olive oil, and beat well with a fork. Season with salt and pepper.

Place the bulgur in a large bowl. Add the parsley, cucumber, tomatoes, green onions, mint, and vinaigrette and stir well, then taste and season with salt and pepper if the salad needs it. Chill before serving.

> **Bulgur is wheat that has been cracked, but it is not cracked wheat. Confused? Well, you're not alone. When wheat berries are cooked, dried, and then cracked with most of the hull removed, they are called bulgur. When wheat berries have been cracked without being cooked or hulled, they are called cracked wheat. Fortunately for us, the hull/no hull decision is easy because true cracked wheat is difficult to find in the United States.**
>
> **food trivia**

4 dinner for one

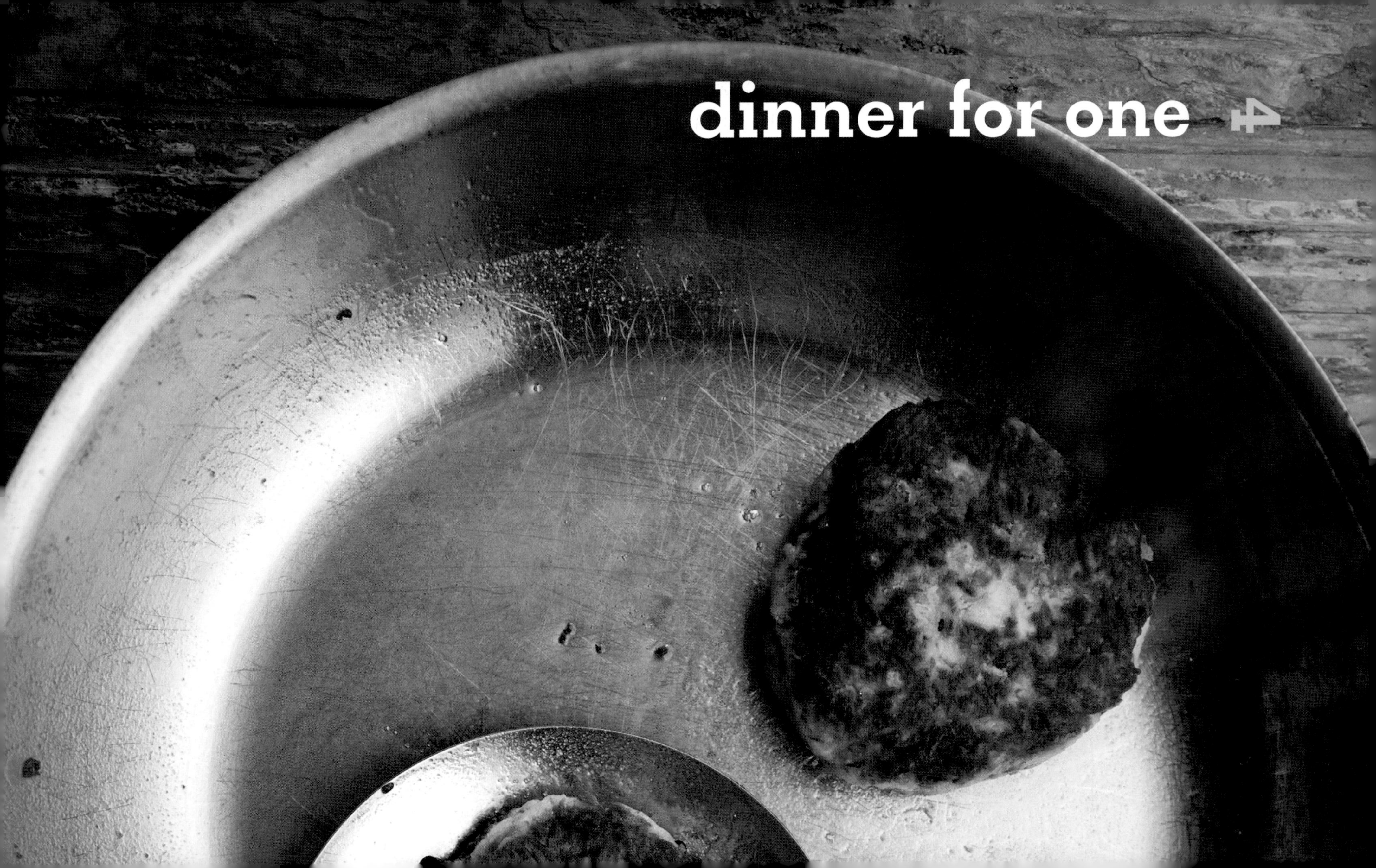

zucchini cakes with horseradish sauce

m : I got the idea for this recipe from a Greek restaurant I worked at. The horseradish sauce is my favorite thing about them because I love that rush of spiciness that clears the sinuses. **Serves 1**

2 green onions

1/4 cup mayonnaise

2 teaspoons horseradish

1 teaspoon milk

1 zucchini

1 small clove garlic

1 egg yolk

1 tablespoon flour, plus about 1/4 cup for dipping

Salt and pepper

1 tablespoon canola oil

Cut off and discard the roots of the green onions, and cut the whites and about 1 inch of the green parts into thin slices. Place half the sliced green onions, the mayonnaise, horseradish, and milk in a small bowl and stir until well combined. Reserve the rest of the sliced green onions.

Cut off the ends of the zucchini and discard. Grate the zucchini and place it on a paper towel. Wrap the paper towel around the zucchini and squeeze over the sink to remove the excess liquid. Peel and finely chop the garlic or pass it through a garlic press.

Lightly beat the egg yolk in a large bowl. Add the reserved green onions, the garlic, and 1 tablespoon of the flour. Gently stir in the zucchini and season with salt and pepper. Put the 1/4 cup of flour into a small, flat dish. Form the zucchini mixture into 2 balls, dip the balls into the dish of flour so that they are coated all over, and flatten them slightly to form the cakes. Heat the canola oil in a large nonstick skillet over medium heat, add the zucchini cakes, and cook for 5 to 7 minutes on each side, or until golden brown.

Place the zucchini cakes on a plate and top with the sauce.

roasted red pepper and avocado wrap

j: In my experience, wraps can go either way: sometimes they completely hit the spot, and other times they're just boring fuel. This one always falls into the former category. Besides the fact that the colors of the food make it pretty (I know that sounds lame, but it's true), the red pepper and avocado are an awesome combination of flavors and textures. It's a little time-consuming to roast the pepper, but it's so delicious that you'll be glad you did it. Plus, you only need half of the pepper for each wrap, so you can store the other half to make another wrap in a jiff within the next few days. **Serves 1**

1 red bell pepper

1/2 avocado

1 (10-inch) flour tortilla

1 teaspoon Dijon mustard

2 slices provolone cheese
(about 2 ounces total)

A small handful (about 1 ounce)
baby spinach leaves

Roast the bell pepper by placing the whole pepper directly on the gas stove burner (if you have an electric stove, do this under the broiler) and cook, turning occasionally, for 10 to 15 minutes, or until it is almost completely black on all sides. Pick it up with some tongs or a fork, place it in a bowl, cover the bowl tightly with plastic wrap, and let it stand for 10 minutes. (The steam will loosen the skin and make it easy to peel off.) Scrape the blackened skin off the pepper with your fingers and discard it, along with the stem and seeds. Cut the pepper into 4 lengthwise strips.

Beginning at the larger end of the avocado half, slide a spoon between the skin and flesh and gently scoop out the flesh in one whole piece. Cut it into 8 slices. Lay the tortilla flat and spread with the mustard. Place the cheese in the center of the tortilla and top with 2 of the bell pepper strips. Place the avocado slices over the bell pepper and arrange a layer of spinach leaves over the avocado. Fold up the bottom edge of the tortilla, then fold in both sides to form the wrap.

 Depending on when you buy them, red bell peppers can cost a few dollars each at their regular price. I buy them when they are in season (summertime) or when they go on sale, and roast and peel a bunch of them at one time. Then I cut them into strips and freeze them in an airtight container with wax paper between the layers of peppers. They'll keep for several months, so you can just take them out as you need them.

bargain shopper

teriyaki portobello sandwich with baked potato wedges

m : I wasn't enthused about this recipe idea and was not particularly happy
when I had to test it. In my opinion, the world didn't need another mushroom burger. But I went to work and was quickly finished. "At least it didn't
take very long," I mumbled. I bit into it, expecting the standard, run-of-the-
mill mushroom burger you get in every restaurant nowadays, but then I
had to pause mid-chew. This was no normal mushroom burger. This—this
was a luau in my mouth! Okay, maybe that's a tiny overstatement, but this
is so easy and good, there's no reason not to make it. **Serves 1**

1 potato

Cooking spray

Salt and black pepper

1 portobello mushroom

2 tablespoons teriyaki sauce

$^1/_2$ onion

2 teaspoons canola oil

1 slice pineapple

1 hamburger bun

Preheat the oven to 400°F.

Slice the potato lengthwise into 8 wedges and place on a baking sheet. Spray lightly with cooking spray and season with salt
and pepper. Bake for 25 to 30 minutes, or until golden brown.

Meanwhile, cut the end off the mushroom stem, discard, and
place the portobello in a shallow bowl. Add the teriyaki sauce,
turn the mushroom to coat it with the sauce, and marinate for
15 minutes.

Peel the onion and cut into thin slices. Heat the oil in a skillet
over medium heat. Add the onion and cook, stirring frequently,
for 10 to 12 minutes, or until translucent. Pour the teriyaki
sauce from the mushroom into the pan and cook for 5 minutes, or until the liquid has been absorbed. Remove the onion
from the pan and set aside.

Add the mushroom to the pan and cook over medium heat for
6 or 7 minutes on each side, or until warm. Add the pineapple
slice to the pan and cook for 1 minute to warm.

Place the portobello on the bottom half of the bun and top
with the pineapple and onions, and then the other half of the
bun. Serve with the potato wedges on the side.

**Portobello mushrooms are just the big bro-
ther of cremini mushrooms. Once a cremini
grows to be more than 4 inches in diameter, it is
deemed to be a portobello.**

cooking 101

daikon radish salad with sesame fried tofu

m : This Japanese spin on coleslaw is a refreshing salad, and serving it with crispy fried tofu coated with sesame seeds makes for a great, quick dinner. Even though the tofu is fried, you only need a little bit of oil, so it's still a nice light meal. **Serves 1**

$1/2$ teaspoon minced fresh ginger

Canola oil

2 teaspoons rice vinegar

1 teaspoon soy sauce

1 small daikon radish

1 carrot

4 ounces extra-firm tofu

1 tablespoon flour

1 tablespoon sesame seeds

Combine the ginger, 1 teaspoon of the canola oil, rice vinegar, and soy sauce in a bowl. Peel the daikon and carrot and cut them into matchstick-sized pieces (about $1/8$ by $1/8$ by 2 inches). Add the daikon and carrot to the bowl and toss well.

Cut the tofu into $3/4$-inch cubes and place on a paper towel. Cover the cubes with another paper towel and gently press on the tofu to remove the excess liquid. Combine the flour and sesame seeds in a shallow bowl, add the tofu cubes, and gently turn to coat with the flour mixture. Pour about $1/2$ inch of oil into a saucepan and place over medium-high heat until very hot. (A tiny drop of water flicked into the pan should immediately cause the oil to bubble up.) Add the tofu cubes to the pan and cook for 1 minute on each side, or until lightly browned.

Place the daikon salad on a plate and top with the fried tofu.

Daikon is a long, white radish that is less spicy than most other radishes. They are generally about 2 inches in diameter and 8 to 14 inches long. They're available in most grocery stores, and they're delicious sliced onto green salads or to give your coleslaw a little extra zip.

cooking 101

white bean salad

m: Okay, this salad is really dinner-for-one-and-lunch-the-next-day. I got the recipe from my host sister in Germany, who says that the longer the salad is in the fridge, the better it tastes. I told her that I don't think we can tell that to college students in the U.S., because some of them will end up with science experiments! Still, you could even make a double or triple batch and keep it in the fridge for a quick lunch or to bring along to a barbecue. **Serves 1 (with leftovers)**

$1/2$ red bell pepper

$1/2$ onion

2 tablespoons olive oil

1 (15-ounce) can white beans

1 tablespoon cider vinegar

Salt and pepper

Remove the stem, seeds, and membranes from the bell pepper, then cut the pepper into $1/4$-inch pieces. Peel the onion and cut into $1/4$-inch pieces. Place 1 tablespoon of the olive oil in a small skillet and add the onion and bell pepper. Cook over medium heat for 8 to 10 minutes, or until the onion is translucent.

Place the beans in a strainer and rinse under cold water. Drain them well, then place them in a bowl and stir in the onion and bell pepper. Stir in the cider vinegar and the remaining 1 tablespoon of olive oil and season with salt and pepper. Eat half now and put the rest in the fridge for later.

There are a zillion types of specialty vinegars on the market today, but we try to limit ourselves to just a few. Balsamic vinegar is dark brown with a full-bodied combination of sweet and sour flavors. It is wonderful for salad dressings, sprinkled on vegetables, or in marinades. Rice wine vinegar is very pale yellow with a mild, delicate flavor that pairs well with herbs or spices. It is used a lot in stir-fries because it doesn't alter the appearance of the food. White wine vinegar is clear and nearly colorless. It is slightly more acidic than rice wine vinegar and is perfect for spicy dishes and marinades. Cider vinegar is a light tan color and has a slight apple flavor. It works well for salad dressings and on vegetables.

cooking 101

maki rolls

j: It can be expensive to buy sushi, but it's pretty cheap to make at home. And it's nice because then you can use whatever vegetables you like, rather than settling for the standard vegetables that are in most rolls. You can use what we've listed here, or pick something completely different. It's up to you. Nori (seaweed sheets), rice vinegar, sushi rice, and wasabi paste are the special ingredients to seek out for this dish. They may all be available in your super-market or natural foods store, or (definitely) in an Asian food store. Bamboo sushi mats are cheap and handy to have if you are going to make maki sushi regularly; they can be found in most kitchenware stores these days. **Serves 1**

1 cup sushi rice

1 1/2 cups water

1 1/2 teaspoons sugar

1 tablespoon rice vinegar

1/4 red bell pepper

1/4 cucumber

4 asparagus spears

2 sheets nori

2 1/2 teaspoons wasabi paste

1/4 cup soy sauce, or more, for dipping

Place the rice and water in a small saucepan and bring to a boil over high heat. Cover and cook over medium-low heat for 15 minutes. Remove from the heat and let cool to room tem-perature. Place the sugar and rice vinegar in a small bowl and stir until the sugar dissolves. Sprinkle the vinegar mixture over the rice and toss well to coat the rice thoroughly.

While the rice is cooking and cooling, prepare the vegetables. Cut the bell pepper into thin strips. Peel the cucumber and cut into long strips about 1/4 to 3/8 inch wide. Break off and discard the tough ends from the asparagus, then place the asparagus in a saucepan wide enough for the spears to lie flat, with about 1 inch of water. Cook over medium-high heat for 5 minutes, or until tender. (Alternatively, if you have a micro-wave, place in a microwave-safe bowl. Add a few tablespoons of water, cover with plastic wrap or wax paper, and microwave on high heat for 3 to 4 minutes, or until barely tender.)

Lay a sheet of nori on a bamboo sushi mat or plastic wrap and spoon on half the rice. Wet your hands to keep the rice from sticking to them, then spread the rice over the nori, leaving a 2-inch border at the top, spreading all the way to the bottom and both sides. Spread 1 teaspoon of the wasabi across the center of the rice. Lay half of the red pepper, cucumber, and asparagus in a row across the center of the rice. Fold the bottom of the mat or plastic wrap up so that the bottom edge of the nori just covers the vegetables. With one hand, pull the mat or plastic gently up from the nori as you roll up the sushi cylinder with the palm of the other hand. Gently press your hands along the roll as you go to create a smooth, firm roll. When the cylinder is rolled, moisten the top border of the nori with a little water and firmly press the edge to seal the roll. Repeat with the remaining ingredients.

Trim the ragged ends from the maki roll with a serrated knife, then cut the roll into 7 or 8 pieces. Combine the soy sauce with the remaining $1/2$ teaspoon of wasabi and stir until combined. Serve the maki rolls with the dipping sauce on the side.

spanikopita

When I've made spanikopita in the past, it's been for appetizers, so I make them a lot smaller. Everyone likes them, but they are incredibly tedious to make. These are bigger and much easier and quicker to make. Just be careful if you happen to be eating them in the car on the way somewhere, because they definitely leave crumbs all over. **Serves 1**

4 ounces frozen chopped spinach, thawed and drained (see page 37)

2 ounces cream cheese, at room temperature

2 ounces feta cheese

1 egg yolk

$1/2$ teaspoon salt

6 sheets frozen phyllo dough, thawed (see Cooking 101, below)

2 tablespoons melted butter

In a bowl, combine the spinach with the cream cheese and mix until smooth. Add the feta cheese, egg yolk, and salt and stir until thoroughly combined.

Preheat the oven to 375°F.

Unroll the phyllo dough, place on a flat surface, and separate out 6 sheets, gently lifting them off the stack of sheets as a single unit. Cover the 6 sheets of phyllo well with barely damp paper towels. (Be sure to cover the phyllo every time you take a sheet or it will dry out.) Return the remaining dough to its packaging, seal tightly, and refrigerate or freeze. Lay 1 sheet of phyllo on a work surface and brush the entire surface with some of the butter. Top with another sheet of phyllo, brush with butter, then top with a third sheet of phyllo. Spoon half of the filling into the center of the pile of buttered phyllo sheets. Fold the sides of the phyllo in over the filling, fold the bottom up, and fold the top down to form a rectangle measuring about 3 by 5 inches. Brush with butter and place fold side down on an ungreased baking sheet. Repeat with the remaining ingredients. Bake for 35 to 40 minutes, or until golden brown. Serve warm or at room temperature.

Phyllo dough isn't difficult to use if you follow a few easy rules. Phyllo should always be defrosted in the refrigerator. Thawing at room temperature causes condensation, which makes the sheets stick together. Make sure the area where you lay the phyllo dough is completely dry; any dampness will cause portions of the dough to stick together. Once the phyllo is unrolled, immediately cover it with a barely damp cloth or paper towel to keep the sheets from drying out.

cooking 101

spanish tortilla

m: I know what you're thinking: "Aren't tortillas those Mexican things that you make quesadillas out of?" Well, yes and no. In Spain, tortilla is an eggy dish a lot like an omelet or a frittata. When I was in Spain, my friend took me out for tapas (Spanish hors d'oeuvres) and one was tortilla. That one was gigantic—really thick, made in big round pans, and sliced for individual servings. Here is a smaller version, but it's just as delicious. It can be served warm or at room temperature. **Serves 1**

1 potato

1/2 onion

1 tablespoon canola oil

Salt and pepper

2 eggs

Traditionally, Spanish tortillas are cooked in copious amounts of olive oil. We have drastically reduced the amount while still using enough to get a great result. But you can even take it a step further; using cooking spray instead of oil saves about 120 calories.

food for thought

Peel and slice the potato and onion about 1/8 inch thick. Heat the oil in a small skillet over medium heat. Add the potato and onion and cook, stirring occasionally, for 12 to 15 minutes, or until the onions are caramelized and the potatoes are tender. Season liberally with salt and pepper.

Beat the eggs well and pour over the potatoes and onions. Cover the pan and cook for 5 minutes, or until a knife inserted into the center of the pan comes out clean. Serve immediately.

soba noodle salad

m : This is one of my favorite salads in the whole book, despite what anyone says about the color. Soba noodles, which are made from buckwheat, are a kind of gray-brown color, so everyone thinks the salad looks a little bizarre or even unappetizing—until they try it and realize that it's a delicious twist on pasta salad. The lime juice and fresh veggies make it refreshing and light. **Serves 1 (with leftovers)**

4 ounces soba noodles

1 tablespoon soy sauce

1 1/2 teaspoons brown sugar

1/2 teaspoon canola oil

1/4 teaspoon curry powder

1 tablespoon peanut butter

1 tablespoon water

1 tablespoon lime juice

3/4 cup snow pea pods

1/4 red bell pepper

1/2 carrot

1 tablespoon finely chopped red onion

Salt and pepper

Bring a large saucepan of salted water to a boil and add the soba noodles. Cook over medium-high heat, stirring occasionally, for 10 minutes, or until al dente. Drain in a colander and rinse with cold water.

While the noodles are cooking, place the soy sauce, brown sugar, canola oil, and curry powder in a bowl and stir until the sugar is dissolved. Stir in the peanut butter, water, and lime juice and mix until well combined.

Cut the snow pea pods into 1-inch pieces on the diagonal. Cut the bell pepper into very thin slices and cut the slices in half lengthwise. Peel the carrot and cut into matchstick-sized pieces (about 1/8 by 1/8 by 2 inches).

Place the soba noodles in a large bowl and add the pea pods, bell pepper, carrot, and red onion. Add the sauce and toss until combined. Season with salt and pepper and refrigerate until ready to serve.

Soba noodles are a gluten-free noodle made from buckwheat flour. Because of their buckwheat content, they're a slow-releasing carbohydrate, which helps keep blood sugar levels stable. They're a staple of Japanese cuisine but don't (yet) have the same following in the U.S.—though they are increasingly available in supermarkets (check the Asian food aisle). Personally, I think that's because of their unusual gray-brown color. I say get over that and give them a try. They're excellent!

cooking 101

broccoli and cauliflower with satay dipping sauce

m : Satay is an Indonesian dish where, typically, foods are skewered and then grilled or broiled. But to me satay is all about the peanut sauce that's served alongside the skewers. I love peanut sauce! I made a stovetop version with just broccoli and cauliflower accompanied with that amazing peanut dipping sauce, so it would be a really easy meal for one. The sauce would also be great with some baked tofu. **Serves 1**

$1/3$ cup creamy peanut butter

1 tablespoon rice vinegar

1 teaspoon soy sauce

1 teaspoon chili paste (see page 44)

1 cup broccoli florets

1 cup cauliflower florets

Place the peanut butter, rice vinegar, soy sauce, and chili paste in a small bowl and stir until combined.

Bring a large saucepan of water to a boil over high heat. Add the broccoli and cauliflower and cook for 3 to 4 minutes, or until they are still firm but also a bit tender. (Alternatively, if you have a microwave, place the broccoli and cauliflower in a microwave-safe bowl and add a little water. Cover with plastic wrap or wax paper and cook on high heat for 3 to 4 minutes, or until just cooked.) Drain in a colander.

Place the broccoli and cauliflower on a plate and serve with the sauce on the side.

> Broccoli and cauliflower are part of the family of cruciferous vegetables, along with cabbage, kale, radishes, bok choy, and about thirty others. They are considered to be superfoods—they are completely packed with nutrients, including fiber and cancer-fighting antioxidants and lots of phytochemicals (aka, chemical compounds found in plants that are believed to benefit human health). In even better news, if you cook them right, they taste good, too.
>
> **food for thought**

egg foo yong

m: I am an egg foo yong connoisseur, so I was completely confused when I tried it here in Phoenix. The egg patties were plain and hard and the vegetables were served on top. I found this so disturbing that for the first few months we lived here I tried every Chinese restaurant in a fifteen-mile radius that was listed in the phone book. None of them served the version I was used to, with the vegetables inside. You know what happened next: I came up with this recipe. **Serves 1**

Gravy

1 vegetable bouillon cube

1 cup water

1 tablespoon soy sauce

1 tablespoon cornstarch

Egg Foo Yong

1 (15-ounce) can mixed Chinese vegetables

2 eggs

1 teaspoon soy sauce

1 teaspoon canola oil

1 cup cooked white rice (see page 6)

To prepare the gravy: Place the bouillon cube and water in a small saucepan and bring to a boil. Combine the soy sauce and cornstarch, stir until smooth, then stir into the bouillon. Cook over medium-high heat for 5 minutes, or until the mixture comes to a full boil. Turn down the heat very low to keep the sauce warm while you finish the dish.

To prepare the egg foo yong: Drain the vegetables well. Place the eggs and soy sauce in a bowl and beat until thoroughly combined. Stir in the vegetables. Heat the canola oil in a small skillet over medium heat. Pour the egg mixture into the pan, cover, and cook for 5 to 7 minutes, or until a knife inserted into the center comes out clean.

Scoop the rice onto a plate, top with the egg foo yong, and pour the gravy over the top.

> **Egg foo yong is a kind of omelet—dry, more like an Italian frittata than a French omelet—filled with veggies and sometimes meat, fried in a pan, and served with gravy. Popular wisdom says it was invented by Chinese-American cooks in the 1930s, but actually it does have genuine Chinese origins. In any case, it is a classic Chinese-restaurant dish in the United States.**
>
> **food trivia**

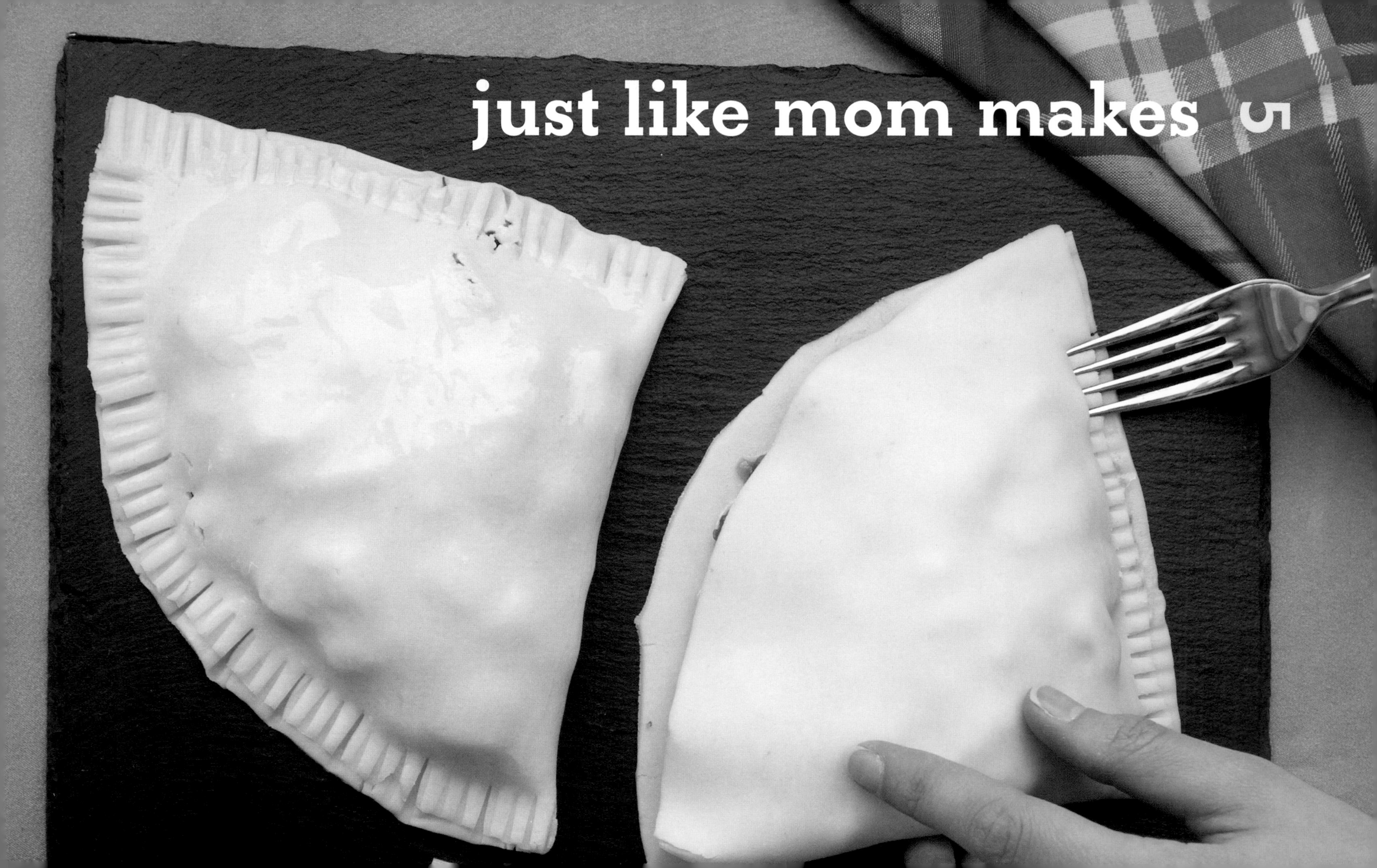

5 just like mom makes

vegetable pot pie

m : No one can deny the comfort food factor associated with a steaming hot pot pie with its crispy crust and delicious sauce. Even if your mom never actually made one for you from scratch, at least she probably bought you frozen ones on occasion. Our version is made with lots of vegetables, and it's a treat for meat eaters and vegetarians alike. **Serves 4**

3 potatoes

2 carrots

1 small onion

8 ounces mushrooms

2 cups water

1 vegetable bouillon cube

1 cup frozen peas

$1/4$ cup flour

$1/2$ teaspoon poultry seasoning

$1/2$ cup milk

Salt and pepper

1 sheet frozen puff pastry, thawed (see page 5)

Preheat the oven to 400°F.

Peel the potatoes and cut into $1/2$-inch cubes. Peel the carrots and cut into $1/4$-inch cubes. Peel the onion and cut into $1/2$-inch pieces. Cut the ends off the mushroom stems, discard, and cut the mushrooms in half.

Place the water, bouillon cube, potatoes, carrots, onion, and mushrooms in a saucepan and bring to a boil. Cover and simmer over medium-low heat for 10 to 12 minutes, or until the potatoes are tender. Add the peas to the pan. In a bowl, combine the flour, poultry seasoning, and milk and stir until smooth. Slowly add the milk mixture to the pan, stirring constantly. Season with salt and pepper and cook over medium heat for 5 minutes, or until the sauce thickens.

Pour the mixture into a 2-quart casserole dish and top with the sheet of puff pastry. Press the pastry down firmly around the outside edge of the dish and cut 4 small slits in the top. Bake for 30 to 35 minutes, or until the puff pastry is golden brown. Serve immediately.

Puff pastry is made up of very thin layers of dough with butter between each layer. The steam caused by the moisture in the butter separates and "puffs" the layers as it bakes. I thought about making puff pastry from scratch once, but quickly changed my mind. The first recipe I looked at said it took 3 days and they got worse from there. Fortunately, the frozen version is readily available and works great.

cooking 101

"Season with salt and pepper" can be frightening words to a novice cook. You immediately start to wonder how much is enough and what is too much. Exact amounts for salt and pepper aren't generally listed because the amount of seasoning needed varies based on the brands and types of ingredients used and on personal taste. The easy answer is to add a little, give it a chance to dissolve, and taste it. Each time you add a little more you should notice a slight difference. The first few times you will probably have to add seasonings over and over until it tastes right, but after a while you will get the hang of how much to start with and it will go much quicker.

cooking 101

butternut squash soup

m: This soup is perfect for a chilly autumn night, when you just want to wrap yourself in a warm blanket and watch television. It is as easy as cutting up the vegetables and waiting for them to cook. And the best part is, because the vegetables get puréed in the end, it doesn't matter how big or small or funny shaped they are. But do be careful not to put too much in the blender at a time, unless you're trying to redecorate your kitchen. **Serves 4**

1 stalk celery

1 small onion

1 carrot

2 potatoes

1 large butternut squash (2 1/2 to 3 pounds)

4 cups water

2 vegetable bouillon cubes

Salt and pepper

Sour cream (optional)

Trim and discard the ends of the celery and cut into 1/2-inch slices. Peel and coarsely chop the onion, carrot, and potatoes. Cut the squash in half across the neck, then put the halves cut side down on the cutting board and cut each half in half. Scoop out the seeds and strings with a spoon. Peel the squash with a vegetable peeler or cut it off with your knife, and cut into 3/4-inch chunks.

Place the celery, onion, carrot, potatoes, squash, water, and bouillon cubes in a large pot and bring to a boil. Simmer over medium-low heat for 25 to 30 minutes, or until all the vegetables are tender.

Ladle some of the vegetables and liquid into a blender (don't fill the blender jar more than halfway) and cover first with the lid, then with a towel. Blending hot soup can cause the top to pop off, making a huge mess and maybe even burning you. Holding the top down tightly, purée the first batch until smooth. Pour the puréed soup into a large bowl and continue puréeing the remaining soup in batches. Pour the soup back into the saucepan and cook over low heat for 5 minutes, or until warm. Season with salt and pepper.

Ladle into bowls and top with a spoonful of sour cream, if desired.

vegetable empanadas

j: You can make these empanadas whatever size you want. If you want to have something a bit more substantial, you can make them bigger and have fewer of them, or you can make them smaller and take them as an appetizer to a party. Either way: yummy. **Serves 4**

2 zucchini

1 onion

2 potatoes

2 tablespoons canola oil

1 (15-ounce) can diced tomatoes

1 teaspoon crushed red pepper

Salt and pepper

2 prepared piecrusts (see page 5)

Preheat the oven to 350°F.

Trim and discard the ends of the zucchini and cut into 1/2-inch pieces. Peel the onion and potatoes and cut into 1/2-inch pieces.

Place the oil in a large nonstick skillet over medium heat. Add the zucchini, onion, and potatoes and cook, stirring occasionally, for 10 minutes, or until the potatoes are tender. Drain the juice from the tomatoes and add them to the pan. Add the crushed red pepper and cook for 5 minutes, or until the tomatoes are warm. Season with salt and pepper.

Lay the piecrusts on a flat surface and cut each one in half. Spoon one-fourth of the vegetable mixture into the center of one half circle of dough. Wet your finger and dampen the entire edge of the dough, then fold the dough over and press all around the edges with a fork to seal. Cut a slit in the top of the dough and place on an ungreased baking sheet. Repeat with the remaining ingredients. Bake for 30 minutes, or until golden brown, and serve immediately.

Here is some silly trivia about onions: Consuming nearly 67 pounds per year, Libyans eat more onions per capita than any other country. In comparison, we Americans gobble down a measly 20 pounds per person each year. My only hope is that they use a proportionate amount of breath mints.

food trivia

barbecue tofu with onion rings

m : The secret to this recipe is the second layer of flour on the tofu. It makes for a nice thick layer of batter that stays crispy even once the barbecue sauce is on it. The tricky part about his recipe is the frying. Even though you only use an inch or two of oil, be sure to use a big, deep pot or pan just in case it splashes, and use a long spoon or spatula, preferably slotted, to turn the onion rings and tofu because it hurts like heck to burn yourself with hot oil. And please don't be scared off by these tips; frying is really pretty easy as long as you take the proper precautions, and your tastebuds will definitely be happy with the end result! **Serves 4**

1 (14-ounce) package extra-firm tofu

2 large onions

1 egg

$1/4$ cup water

2 cups flour

Salt and pepper

Canola oil for frying

$1/2$ cup barbecue sauce

Drain the tofu and cut it into $1/4$-inch-thick slices. Lay the pieces between several paper towels, top with a heavy pan, and let stand for 15 minutes to press out any excess water.

Peel the onions and cut into $1/4$-inch-thick slices. Place the onion rings in ice-cold water until ready to use.

Beat the egg and water together in a shallow bowl. Place 1 cup of the flour in a shallow bowl. Season the flour heavily with salt and pepper and stir it in.

Pour about $1^1/2$ inches of oil into a saucepan and place over medium-high heat until very hot (about 350°F). (A tiny drop of water added to the pan should immediately cause the oil to bubble up.) Dip the tofu into the flour, then the egg, then the flour again. Carefully place the tofu into the oil using a slotted spoon and cook for 4 to 5 minutes, or until golden brown. Remove with a slotted spoon and drain on paper towels.

Remove the onion rings from the water and blot lightly on paper towels. Place the remaining 1 cup of flour into a large resealable bag and add some of the onions. Shake until they are thoroughly coated, then carefully transfer the onions to the hot oil using a slotted spoon. Cook for 10 to 15 minutes, or until golden brown. Remove with a slotted spoon and drain on paper towels. Continue with the remaining onion rings.

Place some of the tofu and onion rings on each plate and spoon the barbecue sauce over the tofu.

The creation of onion rings is apparently a subject of dispute. Some say that they were developed by Pig Stand restaurants in the 1920s and others attribute them to Sam Quigley in the 1950s. Either way, there are enough types of onion rings to go around. Onion rings can be battered, when they are dipped in a thicker, wet sauce, or breaded, when they are rolled in breadcrumbs or flour, like in our recipe.

food trivia

shepherd's pie

j: You're probably skeptical about how such a standard meat and potatoes dish as shepherd's pie could be made vegetarian, but it can definitely be done. This dish is great comfort food—white beans and veggies baked bubbly hot with a golden mashed potato crust. **Serves 4**

2 pounds potatoes

1/2 cup milk

1/4 cup butter

8 ounces mushrooms

1 onion

2 cloves garlic

1 stalk celery

2 carrots

1 cup water

1/2 vegetable bouillon cube

1 (15-ounce) can diced tomatoes

1 (15-ounce) can cannellini beans

1 teaspoon soy sauce

2 tablespoons flour

Salt and pepper

Preheat the oven to 350°F.

Peel the potatoes, cut into large chunks, and place in a large pot of salted water. Bring to a boil and cook over medium heat for 25 to 30 minutes, or until tender. Drain the water and return the potatoes to the pan. Add the milk and butter to the pan and cook over high heat for 4 to 5 minutes, or until the milk comes to a boil. Remove from the heat and smash the potatoes with a potato masher or sturdy fork until fairly smooth.

Meanwhile, cut the ends off the mushroom stems, discard, and cut the mushrooms into quarters. Peel the onion and cut into 1/2-inch pieces. Peel and finely chop the garlic. Trim and discard the ends of the celery and cut into 1/2-inch pieces. Peel the carrots, cut in half lengthwise, and slice about 1/4 inch thick.

$ Shepherd's pie was most likely the invention of frugal British housewives in the eighteenth century looking for a way to use up leftover meat. Even though this version doesn't have meat, the same principle can still apply. This dish calls for specific vegetables, but just about any vegetables will work. Take this as an opportunity to use up some of those leftovers. I figure that no matter what's inside, if it has gravy and is topped with mashed potatoes, it's shepherd's pie.

bargain shopper

Place 3/4 cup of the water and the bouillon cube in a large saucepan and bring to a boil. Add the mushrooms, onion, garlic, celery, and carrots and cook over medium-high heat for 12 to 15 minutes, or until the carrots are tender. Remove the pan from the heat. Drain the tomatoes and add to the pan, then add the cannellini beans with their liquid. In a bowl, combine the soy sauce, flour, and remaining 1/4 cup of water, stir until smooth, then slowly pour this mixture into the pan, stirring constantly. Season with salt and pepper.

Pour the vegetable mixture into an 8-inch square baking pan or casserole. Spoon the mashed potatoes over the vegetables and smooth to cover the entire pan. Bake for 45 to 50 minutes, or until the potatoes are lightly browned. Serve immediately.

cheddar cheese soup with irish soda bread

J: Everyone who has ever tried this says it's spectacular. Even my mom, who doesn't like cheese, likes this soup, which is saying a lot. The soup itself is an awesome combination of cheese and onions. And the soda bread is so nice and crunchy on the outside and squishy on the inside. It's quite perfect. The only proper way to eat this is to dip the bread in the soup, which means it's an excuse to eat a lot of bread. This is a great cold weather food, although sometimes in summer I suffer through eating it with the air-conditioning turned way up. **Serves 4 to 6**

Soda Bread

Oil or cooking spray

$3^1/2$ cups flour

$1/2$ cup uncooked oatmeal

1 teaspoon salt

1 teaspoon baking powder

1 teaspoon baking soda

8 ounces sour cream

$3/4$ cup skim milk

3 tablespoons sugar

5 tablespoons melted butter

Soup

2 onions

$1/4$ cup butter

$1/3$ cup flour

$2^1/2$ cups water

1 vegetable bouillon cube

$2^1/2$ cups milk

Salt and pepper

2 cups grated Cheddar cheese

To prepare the bread: Preheat the oven to 375°F. Lightly coat a baking sheet with oil or cooking spray.

Combine the flour, oatmeal, salt, baking powder, and baking soda in a large bowl. Combine the sour cream, milk, and sugar in another bowl. Add the sour cream mixture to the dry ingredients and mix just until blended. Stir in 4 tablespoons of the melted butter. Turn the dough out onto the prepared baking sheet and shape into a mounded circle about 8 inches in diameter. Brush the top with the remaining 1 tablespoon of melted butter. Bake for 40 to 45 minutes, or until browned. Cool completely before slicing.

To prepare the soup: Peel the onions and cut into thin slices. Melt the butter in a large saucepan, add the onions, and cook, stirring occasionally, over medium heat for 15 to 20 minutes, or until the onions are translucent. Add the flour and cook, stirring constantly, for 1 minute. Stir in the water, bouillon cube, and milk and bring to a boil. Season with salt and pepper and simmer over low heat, stirring frequently, for 5 minutes. Remove from the heat, add the cheese, and stir until completely melted.

Serve the soup immediately with the soda bread on the side.

> **?** Irish soda bread wasn't invented by the Irish. It's actually credited to Native Americans, but by the 1840s baking soda–leavened bread had become popular in Ireland—maybe because yeast was more expensive than soda.
>
> **food trivia**

stuffed shells

j: I love everything about stuffed shells—love to make them, love the aroma as they're baking, and even love waiting for the cheese on top to get brown. And, of course, I love to eat them. Here's the good news: other than the fact that it takes a while to stuff the shells, they're super easy to make. Plus, you can freeze any leftovers for later. **Serves 6**

12 ounces jumbo shell pasta

2 eggs

32 ounces ricotta cheese

1 cup grated Parmesan cheese

1 teaspoon Italian seasoning

1 (26-ounce) jar prepared spaghetti sauce

2 cups grated mozzarella cheese

Preheat the oven to 350°F.

Bring a large pot of salted water to a boil and add the shells. Cook over medium-high heat, stirring occasionally, for 12 minutes, or until al dente. Drain in a colander.

Meanwhile, beat the eggs lightly in a large bowl. Add the ricotta cheese, Parmesan cheese, and Italian seasoning and stir until combined. Spoon some of the filling into each of the pasta shells and place the stuffed shells in a single layer in an ungreased 9 by 13-inch baking pan. Spread the sauce over the shells, then sprinkle with the mozzarella cheese. Bake for 30 to 40 minutes, or until the cheese is melted and beginning to brown on top. Serve immediately.

poached eggs with vegetable hash

m : This is a fine breakfast after a late night out with friends, but it's so good (and good for you) you could really eat it any time of day. The mix of potato, turnip, and red bell pepper along with the sweet taste of corn is a good-looking, great-tasting combination and an excellent way to get a bunch of veggies in at breakfast. **Serves 4**

1 large turnip

1 large potato

1 onion

1 red bell pepper

2 tablespoons canola oil

1 (15-ounce) can corn, drained

Salt and pepper

Cooking spray

1 teaspoon vinegar

8 eggs

Peel the turnip, potato, and onion and cut into $^1/_4$-inch cubes. Cut the bell pepper in half, remove the seeds and membranes, and cut into $^1/_4$-inch pieces.

Place the oil in a large nonstick skillet over medium heat and add the turnip, potato, onion, and bell pepper. Cook, stirring occasionally, for 12 to 15 minutes, or until soft. Add the corn and cook for 10 minutes, or until the potatoes are golden brown. Season with salt and pepper.

Spray a saucepan with cooking spray and fill it halfway with water. Add the vinegar to the pan and bring to a boil, then lower the heat to medium-low. Carefully crack the eggs directly into the water, being sure not to break the yolks, and cook for 4 to 5 minutes, or until the whites are cooked but the yolk is still soft.

Place some of the hash on each of 4 plates and top with 2 poached eggs.

Why the cooking spray and vinegar? If you've ever made poached eggs, you know they leave a thin layer of a cementlike substance around the pan that's almost impossible to get off. Spraying the pan with cooking spray before adding the water completely eliminates that problem. And adding the vinegar to the water helps the egg white hold together by making the outer layer congeal faster.

cooking 101

enchiladas

J: Enchiladas are perfect for a large group because they can be made ahead of time and then baked just before dinnertime. They're very versatile and can be filled with all sorts of vegetables, but this version with corn and green chiles is one of my favorites. **Serves 4 to 6**

1 onion

2 tablespoons butter

3 cups frozen corn kernels

1 teaspoon ground cumin

1 cup sour cream

1 (4-ounce) can chopped green chiles

2 cups mixed grated Cheddar and Jack cheeses

2 cups salsa

12 corn tortillas

Preheat the oven to 350°F.

Peel the onion and chop into 1/2-inch pieces. Place the butter in a large skillet over medium-high heat and add the onion and corn. Cook, stirring frequently, for 10 to 12 minutes, or until the onion is translucent. Remove from the heat and stir in the cumin, sour cream, green chiles, and 1 cup of the cheese.

Spread about one-third of the salsa in the bottom of an ungreased 9 by 13-inch baking pan. Spoon about 1/3 cup of the onion-corn filling into the center of a tortilla, then roll up the tortilla around the filling and place the enchilada in the pan seam side down (to keep it from opening up). Repeat with the rest of the ingredients. Pour the remaining salsa over the enchiladas and sprinkle with the remaining 1 cup of cheese. Bake for 20 to 25 minutes, or until the cheese is melted. Serve immediately.

> **In Spanish, salsa just means "sauce."** In the United States, salsa usually means the spicy accompaniment for chips or various Mexican dishes. There are lots of different styles of salsa (in the U.S. sense), including salsa verde (green—made with tomatillos), salsa cruda or pico de gallo (made with raw vegetables), and salsa taquera (aka, "salsa for tacos"). Red, green, raw, cooked—we like it all!
>
> **food trivia**

lentil and potato salad

j: Lentils get a bad reputation, largely because they can look like lumpy mud, even though they taste really good. This lentil and potato salad is delicious, and because we used yellow lentils, it actually looks pretty, too. This is great to take to a potluck to share with friends. **Serves 4 to 6**

2 pounds red potatoes

1 cup red or yellow lentils, rinsed (see page 21)

1 bunch green onions

2 tablespoons Dijon mustard

3 tablespoons white wine vinegar

1/4 cup olive oil

Salt and pepper

There are many different types of lentils, but the most common are French green, brown, and yellow. French green lentils have a peppery taste, are the most delicate, and hold their shape well, but they take longer to cook than other lentils. The milder brown lentils and the nutty yellow lentils can hold their shape, but only if they aren't overcooked, which makes them mushy. This recipe would be good with any of these lentils. We chose the yellow simply because we like how they look with the potatoes.

cooking 101

Place the potatoes in a pot with salted water to cover and cook over medium heat for 20 to 25 minutes, or until tender. Drain off the water and as soon as the potatoes are cool enough to handle, cut them into 1-inch pieces.

Place the lentils in a saucepan and add enough water to cover them by about 2 inches. Cook over medium heat for 25 to 30 minutes, or until the lentils are barely soft. Drain in a sieve.

Trim the green onions, discarding the ends, and cut the white and about 1 inch of the green part into thin slices. Combine the mustard, vinegar, olive oil, and green onions in a large bowl and stir well. Gently stir in the potatoes and lentils and season with salt and pepper. Serve warm or refrigerate and serve chilled.

food for the masses

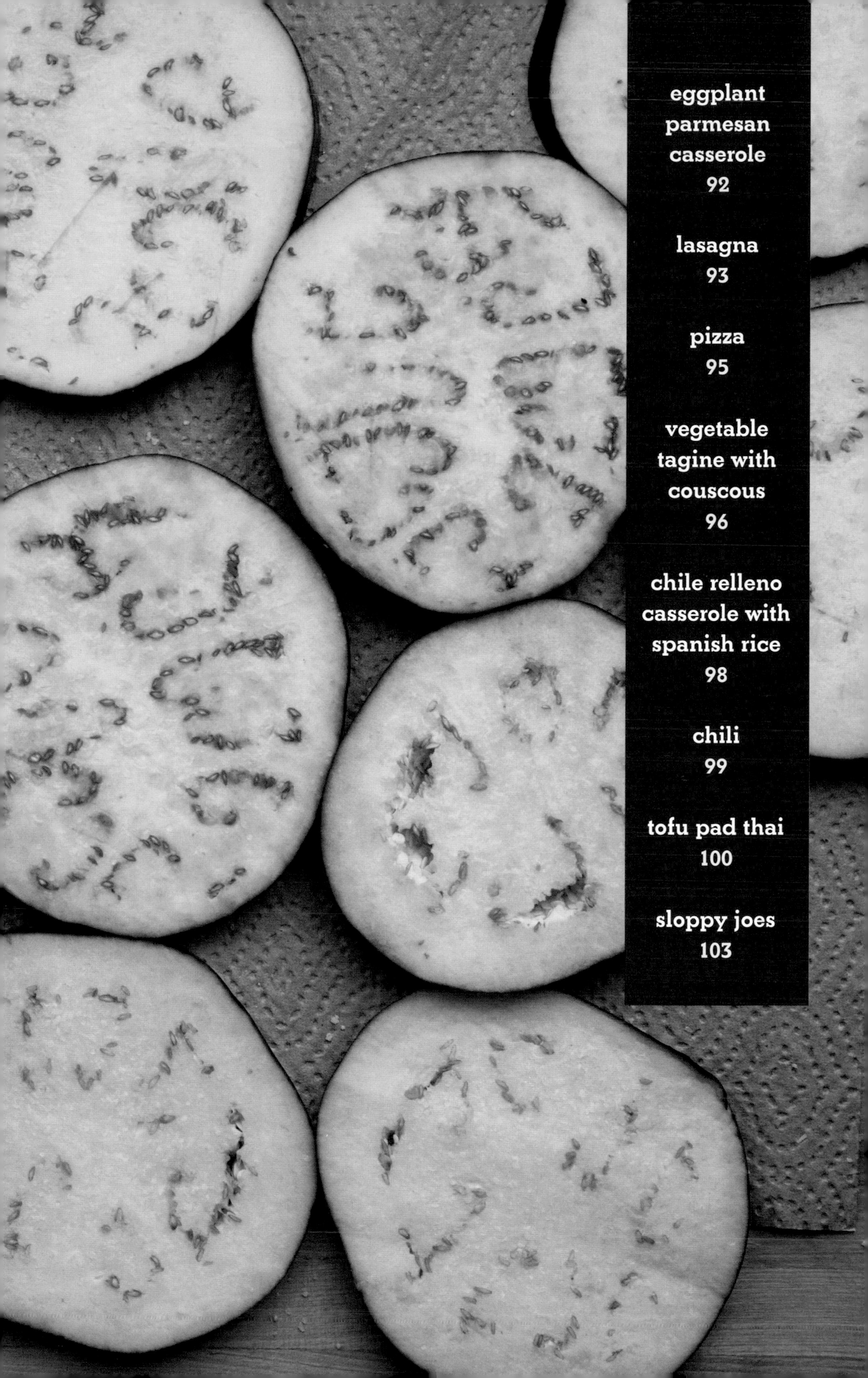

eggplant parmesan casserole

J: Eggplant Parmesan is incredibly delicious, but, in its standard form, pretty labor-intensive. This fun spin on eggplant Parmesan is a great dish to take to a party, or just to make for dinner with friends. Everyone who has ever tried this has asked for more, so you probably won't have leftovers. But that's okay in this case: it's at its best when it's freshly made. **Serves 10 to 12**

2 eggplants

1 egg

$^1/_3$ cup milk

1 cup flour

1 cup breadcrumbs

$^1/_2$ cup canola oil

15 ounces ricotta cheese

$^1/_2$ cup grated Parmesan cheese

1 pound grated mozzarella cheese

1 (26-ounce) jar prepared spaghetti sauce

Preheat the oven to 350°F.

Trim and discard the stem of the eggplants, then cut them lengthwise into $^1/_4$- to $^3/_8$-inch-thick slices. Beat the egg in a shallow bowl, add the milk, and stir until combined. Place the flour and breadcrumbs in separate shallow bowls. Heat 2 tablespoons of the oil in a large skillet over medium-high heat. Dip a slice of the eggplant into the flour, then the egg, then the breadcrumbs and carefully place it in the hot oil using a fork. Repeat until you can't fit any more slices in the skillet in a single layer. Cook for 3 to 4 minutes on each side, or until golden brown, then drain on paper towels. Repeat with the remaining eggplant slices, adding more of the oil as needed.

Combine the ricotta cheese, Parmesan cheese, and 1 cup of the mozzarella cheese in a bowl. Arrange a single layer of cooked eggplant slices in the bottom of an ungreased 9 by 13-inch baking pan. Spread one-third of the ricotta mixture over the eggplant, top with one-third of the spaghetti sauce, and sprinkle with one-third of the remaining mozzarella cheese. Repeat the process until there are 3 complete layers. Bake for 40 to 45 minutes, or until the cheese is bubbly and lightly browned. Let stand for 10 minutes before serving.

? Here's a little plant anatomy 101. Eggplants are fruits, not vegetables, and if you want to get technical about it, they are actually berries. A berry is defined as any type of fleshy fruit that develops from the ovary wall of the plant flower but doesn't sprout open when ripe. So, technically, eggplants, as well as tomatoes, bananas, chile peppers, and avocados, are all berries.

food trivia

lasagna

m: This version of lasagna is really unbeatable, with lots of mushrooms, spinach, and cheese. Use no-cook (or no-boil) lasagna noodles so you don't have to cook them beforehand—they absorb the liquid in the filling and cook as the lasagna bakes. If you're having people over, you can assemble it in advance and keep it in the fridge until you're ready bake it. Serve it with a big salad and garlic bread, and you can practically feed your whole neighborhood. **Serves 10 to 12**

1 pound mushrooms

1 large onion

4 cloves garlic

3 tablespoons canola oil

1 pound frozen chopped spinach

2 eggs

32 ounces ricotta cheese

1 (26-ounce) jar prepared spaghetti sauce

1 (12-ounce) box no-cook lasagna noodles

1 pound grated mozzarella cheese

1 cup grated Parmesan cheese

Preheat the oven to 350°F.

Cut the ends off the mushroom stems, discard, and cut the mushrooms into thin slices. Peel the onion and cut into $1/2$-inch pieces. Peel and finely chop the garlic or pass it through a garlic press.

Place the canola oil in a large skillet over medium-high heat. Add the mushrooms, onion, and garlic and cook, stirring frequently, for 10 to 12 minutes, or until the onion is softened. Add the spinach and cook for 8 to 10 minutes, or until all the liquid has evaporated.

Lightly beat the eggs in a large bowl, then stir in the ricotta cheese.

Place a large spoonful of the spaghetti sauce in the bottom of an ungreased 9 by 13-inch baking pan and spread it around. Place a layer of lasagna noodles over the sauce and top with half of the ricotta mixture. Spread one-third of the spaghetti sauce over the cheese and top with half of the spinach mixture. Sprinkle one-third of the mozzarella and one-third of the Parmesan over the spinach. Continue the layering process with noodles, the remaining ricotta mixture, one-third of the spaghetti sauce, the remaining spinach, and one-third of the mozzarella and Parmesan. Top with a final layer of noodles, the remaining sauce, and the remaining mozzarella and Parmesan.

Cover with aluminum foil and bake for 1 hour. Remove the aluminum foil and bake for 15 to 20 minutes, or until the cheese begins to brown. Remove from the oven and let stand for 15 minutes before serving.

To make garlic bread to go with the lasagna, preheat the oven to 350°F. Take a loaf of fresh, crusty bread and cut into 1-inch slices, but keep in the loaf shape. Brush $1/2$ cup melted butter on the bread slices and sprinkle with a little bit of garlic salt. Place on aluminum foil and wrap the loaf. Bake for 15 minutes.

cooking 101

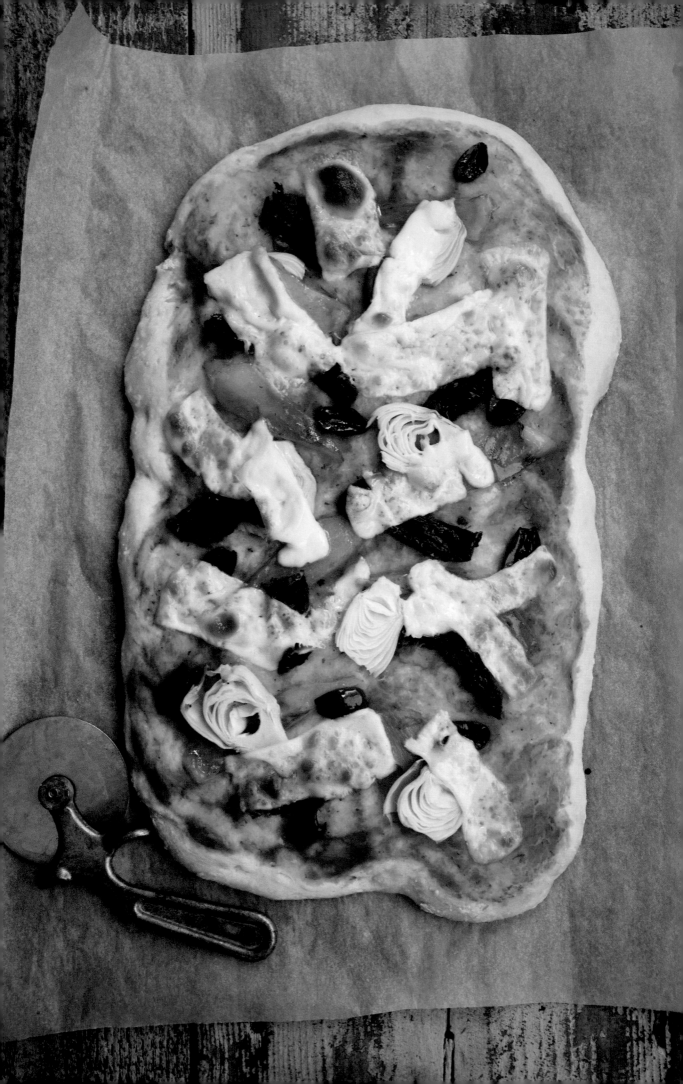

pizza

j: As a college student, you probably donate a large portion of your money to the local pizza chain, especially since it's an easy vegetarian option when you don't feel like cooking. Making your own pizza allows you to be a bit more creative and is way cheaper. This is a perfect version in my book, because you don't have to wait for the crust to rise. Try some soy pepperoni and see if your nonveggie friends notice the difference, or just stick to vegetables. **Makes 2 (8 by 14-inch) pizzas; serves 10**

5 cups all-purpose flour

2 tablespoons sugar

2 ($^1/_4$-ounce) packages active dry yeast

1 teaspoon salt

2 cups warm water (about 105° to 115°F)

$^1/_4$ cup canola oil

3 cloves garlic

1 teaspoon Italian seasoning

1 (15-ounce) can tomato sauce

4 cups topping ingredients (optional)

4 cups grated mozzarella cheese

Preheat the oven to 375°F.

Stir together the flour, sugar, yeast, and salt in a large bowl. Make a well in the center of the flour mixture and add the water and oil. Stir until completely combined. Coat your hands in flour to prevent sticking and spread half of the dough into an 8 by 14-inch rectangle in the center of each of 2 large ungreased baking sheets.

Peel and finely chop the garlic or pass it through a garlic press. Stir the garlic and Italian seasoning into the can of tomato sauce. Spread half of the sauce onto each crust. Spread the topping ingredients over the sauce and sprinkle with the mozzarella cheese. Bake for 20 to 25 minutes, or until the crust is golden brown.

Pineapple, olives, peppers, mushrooms, spinach—everyone has his or her favorite pizza toppings. Most are pretty self-explanatory, but any vegetables should be cleaned before you use them. They should also be chopped fairly thin so that they cook all the way through by the time the rest of the pizza is ready. Make Hawaiian-style pizza with diced pineapple and soy ham or try a more authentic Italian pizza with ricotta cheese, spinach, fresh basil, and tomato.

cooking 101

vegetable tagine with couscous

j: I used to be very apprehensive about different ethnic foods until I studied abroad. The first time I had a tagine was in France and I wondered where it had been all my life! That first tagine was the furthest thing from being vegetarian-friendly, as it came with every kind of meat you can imagine, but an all-vegetable version is just as good. This is a great meal for when you have friends coming over or to take to a potluck. **Serves 10**

1 large onion

2 cloves garlic

2 carrots

3 zucchini

3 yellow squash

1 green bell pepper

2 eggplants

1 tablespoon canola oil

1 teaspoon ground cumin

$1/4$ teaspoon cinnamon

1 teaspoon crushed red pepper

1 teaspoon salt

$3^1/2$ cups water

$1/2$ cup raisins

1 (15-ounce) can diced tomatoes

1 (15-ounce) can chickpeas

$2^1/2$ cups uncooked couscous

Peel the onion and cut into $1/4$-inch pieces. Peel and finely chop the garlic or pass it through a garlic press. Peel the carrots and cut into $1/8$-inch-thick slices. Trim the ends of the zucchini and yellow squash and discard. Cut them in half lengthwise and slice widthwise into $1/4$-inch-thick pieces. Cut the bell pepper in half, remove the seeds and membranes, and cut into $1/2$-inch pieces. Peel the eggplants and cut into $1/2$-inch cubes.

Place the oil in a large saucepan over medium heat. Add the onion and garlic and cook, stirring occasionally, for 3 minutes. Add the carrots, zucchini, squash, bell pepper, cumin, cinnamon, crushed red pepper, salt, and 1 cup of the water and cook, stirring occasionally, for 5 minutes. Stir in the eggplant, the raisins, the tomatoes with their juice, and the chickpeas with their liquid. Cover and cook over medium-low heat, stirring occasionally, for 25 to 30 minutes, or until the vegetables are tender.

Meanwhile, bring the remaining $2^1/2$ cups of water to a boil. Stir in the couscous, cover, and remove from the heat. Let stand for 5 minutes, then fluff with a fork.

Spoon some of the couscous into the center of each plate and top with the vegetable tagine.

A tagine is a Moroccan stew named after the special pot in which it's cooked. A traditional tagine pot is made of heavy clay and consists of a base that's circular and flat with low sides, and a large cone-shaped cover that rests inside the base during cooking. The design of the cover returns the condensation to the bottom. The cover is removed and the base is taken to the table for serving.

cooking 101

chile relleno casserole with spanish rice

m: Although this isn't chile rellenos in their traditional form, it's actually even better because it's way easier and just as tasty. This is good for parties because you can make everything ahead of time, then just put the casserole in the oven and reheat the rice before serving. **Serves 10 to 12**

Casserole

Oil or cooking spray

2 (27-ounce) cans whole green chiles

4 cups mixed grated Cheddar and Jack cheeses

3 eggs

2 tablespoons flour

1 1/2 cups milk

Rice

1 large onion

3 cloves garlic

2 tablespoons canola oil

2 (15-ounce) cans diced tomatoes

2 teaspoons Mexican seasoning

2 cups white rice

4 cups water

To prepare the casserole: Preheat the oven to 350°F. Lightly coat a 9 by 13-inch baking pan with oil or cooking spray.

Drain the chiles, slice them open lengthwise, and arrange them in a single layer in the bottom of the prepared pan. Sprinkle with one-third of the cheese, then cover with another layer of chiles. Sprinkle another one-third of the cheese over the chiles, cover with a final layer of chiles, and top with the remaining cheese.

Separate the egg whites from the yolks and place in separate bowls. Beat the egg whites with a whisk until stiff. Add the flour to the egg yolks and stir until smooth. Slowly pour the milk into the egg yolks, stirring constantly until completely incorporated. Slowly fold the egg yolk mixture into the egg whites until fairly well combined. Spread the egg mixture over the cheese and bake for 45 to 50 minutes, or until lightly browned. Remove from the oven and let stand for 5 minutes before cutting.

To prepare the rice: Peel and coarsely chop the onion. Peel and finely chop the garlic, or pass it through a garlic press.

Heat the oil in a large skillet over medium-high heat. Add the onion and garlic and cook for 10 minutes, or until the onion is translucent. Add the tomatoes with their juice, Mexican seasoning, rice, and water and stir well. Cover and cook over medium-low heat for 20 to 25 minutes, or until the rice is tender and the liquid has been absorbed.

Serve pieces of the casserole with the rice alongside.

Chiles rellenos is a traditional Mexican dish of poblano or Anaheim peppers stuffed with meat, vegetable, or cheese filling (or a combination). Sometimes they're deep-fried, sometimes they're baked, and sometimes they're served "en nogada"— with creamy walnut sauce.

food trivia

chili

m: This version of vegetarian chili uses textured vegetable protein as a substitute for the ground beef. Although it looks a little like granola in its dry form, it absorbs the flavor of whatever you put in the dish, so in the end even meat eaters don't realize it's not really beef. **Serves 10**

1 large onion

3 stalks celery

1 red bell pepper

1 tablespoon canola oil

$1/4$ cup chili powder

2 (15-ounce) cans kidney beans

3 (15-ounce) cans diced tomatoes

3 cups textured vegetable protein

4 cups water

Salt and pepper

Peel the onion and cut into $1/2$-inch pieces. Trim and discard the ends of the celery and cut into $1/2$-inch pieces. Cut the bell pepper in half, remove the seeds and membranes, and cut into $3/8$-inch pieces.

Place the oil in a large sauce pot over medium heat. Add the onion, celery, and bell pepper and cook for 12 to 15 minutes, or until the onion is translucent. Add the chili powder, kidney beans with their liquid, tomatoes with their liquid, textured vegetable protein, and water and stir well. Cook for 30 minutes. Season with salt and pepper and serve immediately.

Textured vegetable protein (made from soybeans) is very high in protein, with each ounce containing 15 grams of protein but only $1/3$ gram of fat. Because it is has little flavor of its own, it's best in very flavorful dishes, such as this chili. You can find it in the bulk section of most produce or natural food stores.

food for thought

tofu pad thai

m: I have loved pad Thai ever since high school when my friends and I found this great Thai restaurant that we went to every chance we got. I have found that making it at home is a more than satisfactory substitute (and, of course, way cheaper). I like to make it spicier and add a little soy sauce, so start out with the recipe here, and then add your own personal touch—that's what cooking is all about anyway! You'll see that the recipe calls for vegetarian fish sauce, which may seem like a funny concept, but you can find it online or at some Asian markets (where you can also pick up the rice noodles). **Serves 10**

2 (12-ounce) packages extra-firm tofu

6 cloves garlic

1 bunch green onions

3/4 cup vegetarian fish sauce

2 cups water

1/3 cup lime juice

1 tablespoon rice vinegar

1/3 cup sugar

1 teaspoon salt

1 teaspoon crushed red pepper

24 ounces rice noodles

4 eggs

3 tablespoons canola oil

4 cups bean sprouts

1/2 cup chopped cilantro

1 cup chopped salted peanuts

Drain the tofu and cut into 1/4-inch-thick slices. Place the pieces between several paper towels, top with a heavy pan, and let stand for 15 minutes to press out any excess water.

Peel and finely chop the garlic or pass it through a garlic press. Trim the green onions, discarding the ends, and cut the white and about 1 inch of the green part into thin slices.

Combine the fish sauce, water, lime juice, rice vinegar, sugar, salt, and crushed red pepper in a bowl, stir well, and set aside.

Bring a large pot of salted water to a boil and add the rice noodles. Cook over medium-high heat, stirring occasionally, for 8 minutes, or until al dente. Drain in a colander.

Meanwhile, lightly beat the eggs. Heat 2 tablespoons of the oil in a large skillet or wok over medium-high heat, add the tofu and cook, stirring occasionally, for 4 to 5 minutes, or until lightly browned. Remove from the pan and set aside. Add the remaining 1 tablespoon of oil to the pan, then add the eggs and cook, stirring frequently, for 2 to 3 minutes, or until the eggs are completely cooked. Remove from the pan and set aside. Add the noodles, garlic, and fish sauce mixture to the pan and cook, stirring constantly, for 2 minutes. Add the eggs, tofu, bean sprouts, green onion, and cilantro and cook, stirring frequently, for 3 to 4 minutes, or until warm. Place in a large serving bowl and top with the chopped peanuts.

sloppy joes

j: In my family, I'm the sloppy joe guru. I stand there for a ridiculously long time adding a little bit of this and a little bit of that, getting the taste just right. Needless to say, I was skeptical about a veggie version. What are sloppy joes without the beef? Well, I can tell you with confidence that they are amazing. In fact, no one even realizes that they don't have meat in them. **Serves 12**

1 large onion

4 stalks celery

1 green bell pepper

1 tablespoon canola oil

2 (6-ounce) cans tomato paste

1 cup ketchup

2 tablespoons prepared yellow mustard

2 tablespoons firmly packed brown sugar

2 cups textured vegetable protein

4 cups water

Salt and pepper

12 hamburger buns

Peel the onion and cut into $1/4$-inch pieces. Trim and discard the ends of the celery and cut into $1/4$-inch pieces. Cut the bell pepper in half, remove the seeds and membranes, and cut into $1/4$-inch pieces.

Place the oil in a large skillet over medium heat. Add the onion, celery, and green pepper and cook, stirring frequently, for 10 to 12 minutes, or until the onion is translucent. Stir in the tomato paste, ketchup, mustard, and brown sugar and cook for 5 minutes. Add the textured vegetable protein and water and stir well. Cook over medium heat for 10 to 12 minutes, or until the water is completely absorbed. Season with salt and pepper.

Spoon the sloppy joes onto the buns and serve immediately.

The substances that give onions their flavor are also the culprits that make you cry when you are cutting them. Onions contain sulfuric compounds that are released when the onion is cut. The chemical is then dissolved in the water in your eyes, creating a mild sulfuric acid. That's right: sulfuric acid. In your eyes. So how can you stop it? Chilling onions before cutting them seems to help some, but sadly, the perfect onion-cutting protectant has not yet been discovered.

cooking 101

bruschetta with fresh mozzarella

j: Bruschetta is a version of garlic bread (garlic toast, really), which is good by me because I think garlic should be its own food group. It's great in just about everything. Fresh mozzarella is the stuff that comes in little round tubs of brine, not the stuff that comes shrink-wrapped and that you put on pizza. It's soft and creamy and tastes amazing with the crispy bread, garlic, tomatoes, and basil. **Makes about 40 pieces**

1 (1-pound) French baguette

1/4 cup olive oil

4 cloves garlic

8 ounces fresh mozzarella cheese

4 tomatoes

1 (2/3-ounce) package basil

Salt and pepper

Preheat the oven to 375°F.

Cut the baguette into 1/4- to 3/8-inch-thick slices and place on a baking sheet. Brush the bread with the olive oil and bake for 10 to 12 minutes, or until light brown. Peel one of the cloves of garlic and rub it over the warm bread slices.

Cut the mozzarella into 1/4-inch cubes. Cut the tomatoes in half, remove the seeds by scraping them out of the tomato with a small tool or your finger, and dice into 1/4-inch pieces. Coarsely chop the basil. Peel and finely chop the remaining 3 cloves of garlic or pass them through a garlic press.

Combine the mozzarella, tomatoes, basil, and chopped garlic in a bowl and season with salt and pepper.

Spoon some of the tomato mixture onto each piece of toasted bread and serve immediately.

$ You may wonder where to find fresh mozzarella cheese. Many grocery stores now have self-serve olive bars that often include fresh mozzarella; otherwise, check the deli counter. They usually have fresh mozzarella that's quite a bit cheaper than prepackaged versions. Plus, you can get exactly the amount you need.

bargain shopper

"bacon" and broccoli quiche

m : Quiche is perfect party food. You can put in any kind of vegetables for filling, and it can be served warm or at room temperature. If you make this in an 8-inch square baking pan, you can cut it into squares for easier serving. **Makes 1 quiche**

2 cups broccoli florets

6 eggs

1 cup evaporated milk

1 1/2 cups mixed grated Cheddar and Jack cheeses

1/4 cup imitation bacon bits

1/2 teaspoon salt

1 prepared piecrust (see page 5)

Preheat the oven to 325°F.

Place a large saucepan with 1 inch of water over high heat and bring to a boil. Add the broccoli to the pan, cover, and cook for 4 minutes, or until tender. Drain the water. (Alternatively, if you have a microwave, place the broccoli in a microwave-safe container and add a little water. Cover with plastic wrap or wax paper and microwave on high heat for 5 minutes, or until tender.)

Whisk together the eggs and evaporated milk in a large bowl. Stir in the cheese, broccoli, bacon bits, and salt.

Press the piecrust into an ungreased 9-inch pie or tart pan. Using a fork, press the tines into the crust around the rim to make a simple pattern. Pour the egg mixture into the crust and bake for 30 to 35 minutes, or until lightly browned and set in the center. Remove from the oven and cool completely. Cut into wedges or squares just prior to serving.

> **$** Okay, this may seem obvious, but I'll mention it anyway. Store-brand piecrusts are substantially cheaper than the name brands, and they're usually just as good. **bargain shopper**

caramelized onion tart

j: One taste of this and you will be hooked. The caramelized onions are so sweet that this could practically be a dessert. Other than the onions taking a while to caramelize, it's so easy to put together, too. Be sure to let it cool completely, and then use a really sharp knife when cutting it so the squares come out clean. **Makes about 60 pieces**

1 prepared piecrust (see page 5)

3 large onions

2 tablespoons butter

Salt and pepper

3 egg yolks

1 (12-ounce) can evaporated milk

Preheat the oven to 375°F. Press the piecrust into an ungreased 8-inch square baking pan.

Peel the onions, cut them in half, then cut into thin slices. Place the butter in a large skillet over medium heat and add the onions. Cook, stirring occasionally, for 25 to 30 minutes, or until the onions are golden brown and caramelized. Spread the onions evenly over the piecrust and season with salt and pepper.

Beat the egg yolks slightly, then mix in the evaporated milk. Pour over the onions and bake for 20 to 25 minutes, or until set in the center. Remove from the oven and cool completely. Cut into 1-inch squares just prior to serving.

Caramelizing onions takes a while but is well worth the effort. Cooking the onions slowly allows them to release their sugar and become golden brown and sweet. And on a completely different note, evaporated milk is just milk with 60 percent of the water removed. Don't confuse it with sweetened condensed milk, which is milk cooked down with added sugar.

cooking 101

focaccia with tomatoes and roasted garlic

m : What is focaccia really? Is it pizza? Is it bread? Well, it's a little bit of both. This version of focaccia is definitely a crowd-pleaser. Just stand back and watch people's eyes light up as they get the zip from the crushed red pepper. That, along with the subtle taste of the roasted garlic, makes this a perfect food to share—just make sure whoever you talk to eats some of it, too. **Makes about 45 pieces**

2 cups warm water (105°F to 115°F)

2 (1/4-ounce) packages dry quick-rising yeast

1 tablespoon sugar

1 teaspoon salt, plus more for sprinkling

4 tablespoons olive oil

4 to 4 1/2 cups flour, plus extra for kneading

Oil or cooking spray

15 cloves garlic

1 (2/3-ounce) package basil

2 large, firm tomatoes

1 teaspoon crushed red pepper

4 slices provolone cheese (about 4 ounces)

Stir together the water, yeast, and sugar in a large bowl and let stand for 5 minutes, or until foamy. Stir in 1 teaspoon of the salt and 2 tablespoons of the olive oil. Gradually add the flour until the mixture forms a soft dough.

Lightly sprinkle a work surface with flour and place the dough in the center. Before kneading the dough, dip your hands in flour to keep them from sticking to the dough. To knead, fold the dough in half and push forward on it slightly with the heels of your hands. Rotate the dough a quarter turn, and again fold it in half, then push on it with the heels of your hands. Continue the turn, fold, and push process for 5 minutes, or until the dough is smooth and elastic. Along the way, dust the dough and the work surface with flour as necessary to keep the dough from sticking. You may need as much as 1 cup of additional flour.

Coat a large bowl with oil or cooking spray. Shape the dough into a ball and place it in the bowl, rolling the ball around in the bowl to lightly coat it with oil. Place the bowl in a warm spot, cover with a kitchen towel, and let rise for 45 minutes, or until almost double in size.

continued

Early versions of focaccia were cooked on the hearth of a hot fire or on a heated tile. It's always had a range of inventive toppings, including herbs, garlic, and onion, but crispy ciccioli, which is the leftovers from rendering chopped-up pork fat into lard, might be a step too far.

food trivia

foccacia with tomatoes and roasted garlic, continued

Lightly coat an 11 by 17-inch baking sheet with oil or cooking spray. Place the dough on the baking sheet and gently pull out the dough until it fills the entire pan in a fairly even layer. Sprinkle lightly with salt and let rise for 30 minutes.

While the dough is rising, roast the garlic. Preheat the oven to 400°F. Peel the garlic and place on a 12-inch piece of aluminum foil. Pull up the ends of the foil to form a pouch and add the remaining 2 tablespoons of olive oil. Fold over the ends of the foil to seal the pouch and bake for 25 to 30 minutes, or until the garlic is soft. Leave the oven on. Place the garlic and oil in a bowl and smash with a fork. Spread the roasted garlic over the dough.

Coarsely chop the basil leaves and sprinkle over the garlic. Cut the tomatoes in half, remove the seeds by scraping them out of the tomato with a small tool or your finger, and cut the tomato into thin slices. Arrange the tomato slices evenly over the dough. Sprinkle the crushed red pepper over the tomatoes. Tear each of the provolone slices into 5 or 6 pieces and arrange them over the tomatoes. Bake the focaccia for 30 to 40 minutes, or until golden brown. Remove from the oven and let cool in the pan. Cut into 2-inch squares and serve.

eggplant tart

j: My roommate recently made this for a party we were having and was surprised that something so tasty and fancy looking could be so easy to make. Everyone loved it and was impressed that she had made it. It travels well, too. Combined with a side salad, it makes for a nice lunch. **Makes about 36 pieces**

Oil or cooking spray

1 eggplant

2 tablespoons canola oil

Salt and pepper

1 sheet frozen puff pastry, thawed (see page 5)

$1/2$ cup ricotta cheese

$1/4$ cup pine nuts

Preheat the oven to 375°F. Lightly coat a baking sheet with oil or cooking spray.

Trim and discard the stem of the eggplant, then cut it into $1/4$- to $3/8$-inch-thick slices. Heat 1 tablespoon of the oil in a large skillet over medium-high heat, add half of the eggplant slices, and season with salt and pepper. Cook for 5 minutes on each side, or until tender. Repeat with the remaining oil and eggplant.

Lay the puff pastry sheet flat on the baking sheet and spread with the ricotta cheese, leaving a $3/4$- to 1-inch border around the edges. Arrange the eggplant over the cheese, sprinkle with the pine nuts, and season with salt and pepper. Bake for 40 to 45 minutes, or until the pastry is golden brown. Cut into $1 1/2$-inch squares and serve warm or at room temperature.

The eggplant is a member of the Solanaceae, or nightshade, family. Its close relatives are potatoes, tomatoes, and peppers. First cultivated in India, eggplant was thought to be poisonous because many members of the nightshade family have large amounts of alkaloids, which can be fatal in large amounts. Although the standard purple oval-shaped eggplant is available in the U.S., there are many other varieties available in Asia and India. They can be green, white, reddish, or dark purple and are often much smaller and thinner than the large American eggplant.

food trivia

potato skins stuffed with green chiles, cheddar, and smashed avocado

m: I stole this version of potato skins from one of my favorite bars near my university. They use green chiles and serve them with ranch dressing. I decided a variation using avocado would be even better, and it is. Don't get me wrong, I love ranch dressing, but this cheese, potato, and avocado combination can't be beat! **Makes 12 potato skins**

6 potatoes

1 green onion

1 clove garlic

1 avocado

2 tablespoons sour cream

1 tablespoon lime juice

1 tablespoon chopped cilantro

2 tablespoons canola oil

2 (4-ounce) cans green chiles

1 1/2 cups grated Cheddar cheese

Preheat the oven to 375°F.

Wash the potatoes and poke each one several times with a fork. Bake for 45 minutes, or until fairly soft when squeezed. Remove the potatoes from the oven and let them cool slightly. Adjust the oven to the broiler setting and place an oven rack 4 to 5 inches away from the broiler.

Meanwhile, trim the green onion, discarding the ends, and cut the white and about 1 inch of the green part into thin slices. Peel and finely chop the garlic, or pass it through a garlic press. Cut the avocado in half, remove the pit, and scoop the flesh into a bowl. Smash the avocado with a fork, add the green onion, garlic, sour cream, lime juice, and cilantro, and stir well. Cover with plastic wrap and refrigerate until ready to serve.

Cut each potato in half lengthwise and scoop out most of the flesh with a large spoon. (Store it in the refrigerator and use it for something else, like mashed or fried potatoes.) Brush the potato skins inside and out with the oil and place skin side up on a baking sheet. Broil for 5 minutes, then turn the potato skins over and broil for 5 to 6 minutes more, or until the potato skins are crispy.

Remove the pan from the oven and spoon some of the green chiles into each potato skin. Top with some of the cheese and return to the broiler for 2 minutes, or until the cheese is melted.

Serve the potato skins on a plate with the smashed avocado on the side.

No way could this be construed as a low-cal recipe, but even small changes can help. If you spray the potato skins with cooking spray instead of using canola oil, you'll save 20 calories per potato skin. Although it may not seem like much, it has no effect on the flavor and it's easier, so why not?

food for thought

oven-fried zucchini sticks with honey mustard sauce

m: This dish is like fried zucchini—minus the actual frying, but just as delicious. The zucchini are super simple to prepare, and you don't have to worry about last-minute preparation because once they come out of the oven, they're finished. I especially love the recipe we came up with for the sauce. It really tastes like what you would get in a restaurant. **Makes about 60 sticks**

Zucchini Sticks

Cooking spray or oil

3 zucchini

$1/2$ cup flour

Salt and pepper

$1 1/2$ cups breadcrumbs

2 eggs

2 tablespoons water

Sauce

$1/2$ cup mayonnaise

1 tablespoon Dijon mustard

2 tablespoons honey

To make the zucchini sticks: Preheat the oven to 400°F. Coat a baking sheet with cooking spray or oil.

Trim and discard the ends of the zucchini. Cut the zucchini in half crosswise, then cut each half into $1/4$-inch-thick sticks.

Place the flour in a resealable bag and season with salt and pepper. Place the breadcrumbs in a shallow bowl. Combine the eggs and water in another shallow bowl and beat well.

Place the zucchini in the bag with the flour and shake well to coat. Dip a piece of the floured zucchini in the egg and then the breadcrumbs, then place on the prepared baking sheet. Repeat with the remaining zucchini. Generously spray the zucchini with cooking spray and bake for 30 to 35 minutes, or until golden brown.

To make the sauce: Combine the mayonnaise, mustard, and honey in a small bowl and stir until smooth.

Serve the zucchini hot out of the oven with the sauce alongside as a dip.

> Here is an appetizer you can dig into without blowing your calorie budget. If you make the sauce with low-fat mayonnaise, 10 zucchini sticks with 2 tablespoons of sauce adds up to less than 240 calories. **food for thought**

zucchini rolls with goat cheese

m: Here's another recipe Jill and I discovered in France (you know how they love their cute little finger foods). These rolls are light and refreshing, making them great for parties, barbecues, or picnics—anywhere you need something that's easy to transport and fun to eat. **Makes about 40 rolls**

2 cloves garlic

5 ounces soft goat cheese

1 tablespoon chopped chives

2 zucchini

Peel and finely chop the garlic, or pass it through a garlic press. Place the garlic, goat cheese, and chives in a small bowl and stir well.

Cut the ends off the zucchini and discard. Using a vegetable peeler, peel one side of the zucchini until the flat section is about 3/4 inch wide; discard the peelings. Pressing firmly on the vegetable peeler, peel long, complete strips off of the zucchini. (The strips should have a strip of green skin on both sides.) Spread some of goat cheese mixture on each strip and roll into a spiral. Refrigerate until ready to serve.

> **Goat cheese is often called chèvre, which is the French word for goat. It is available in a soft creamy version that is similar in consistency to cream cheese, which is perfect for recipes like this one where you want to spread it. It also comes in a dry, semi-firm type that is delicious crumbled on top of salads or pasta dishes.**
>
> **cooking 101**

vegetable pot stickers

j: I've always loved pot stickers, but I was skeptical when we decided to try a vegetarian version. We got it right on the first try, and that doesn't happen often. Your meat-eating friends won't even care that these are vegetarian, because they're pretty darn good dumplings, if I do say so myself. **Makes about 30 pot stickers**

Pot Stickers

1/2 small red onion

8 ounces mushrooms

2 tablespoons canola oil

1 tablespoon minced fresh ginger

2 cups shredded cabbage

Salt and pepper

30 (3-inch) wonton wrappers

Dipping Sauce

2 green onions

2 tablespoons soy sauce

1 tablespoon rice vinegar

1 teaspoon canola oil

To prepare the pot stickers: Peel the onion, cut it in half, then cut it into thin slices. Cut the ends off the mushroom stems, discard, and cut the mushrooms into thin slices.

Heat 1 tablespoon of the oil in a large skillet over medium-high heat. Add the onion, mushrooms, ginger, and cabbage and cook, stirring frequently, for 10 minutes, or until the cabbage is soft. Season with salt and pepper.

continued

vegetable pot stickers, continued

Lay a wonton wrapper on a work surface, dip your finger in water, and wet the entire edge of the wrapper. Place a small spoonful of the cabbage mixture in the center and fold the wrapper in half to enclose the mixture. Firmly press the edges to seal, and just before you seal it completely, push gently around the filling to remove any air pockets. Repeat the process with the remaining ingredients. Lay the finished pot stickers on a baking sheet, keeping them separate so they don't stick together.

Bring a large pot of salted water to a boil. Carefully lower a few of the pot stickers into the water using a slotted spoon and cook for 2 to 3 minutes, or until they float to the top. Remove the pot stickers with the slotted spoon and place on the baking sheet.

Heat the remaining 1 tablespoon of oil in a large nonstick skillet over medium-high heat. Place some of the pot stickers in the pan in a single layer and cook for 2 to 3 minutes, or until golden brown on one side, then transfer to a serving plate and repeat the process with the remaining pot stickers.

To prepare the sauce: Trim the green onions, discarding the ends, and cut the white and about 1 inch of the green part into thin slices. Place the soy sauce, rice vinegar, and canola oil in a small bowl and stir well. Sprinkle with the green onions.

Serve the pot stickers hot, with the sauce alongside.

> Ancient Romans celebrated the medicinal qualities of cabbage. They believed that it should be eaten raw with vinegar. (Can you say coleslaw?) They also liked to make a poultice of raw cabbage paste, place it in a cabbage leaf, and wrap it around an inflamed area to reduce the discomfort. Maybe this worked because it smelled so bad people forgot about the pain.
>
> **food trivia**

artichoke dip

m : Oh my gosh, this artichoke dip is so good! I know that everyone and their mom is making artichoke dip nowadays, but one bite of this and you'll agree it's something special. Even my mom, who doesn't like the two main ingredients—cheese and artichokes—likes it. It's actually a recipe I got from my cousin, with a couple of tweaks. She makes it for any get-together she has at her place and it's always a hit. **Makes about 4 cups**

1 (14-ounce) can artichoke hearts

1 clove garlic

1 cup frozen chopped spinach

1 cup mayonnaise

1 cup grated mozzarella cheese

1 cup grated Parmesan cheese

1 tablespoon minced onion

Crackers or pita chips

Preheat the oven to 350°F.

Drain the artichoke hearts and chop into 1/2-inch pieces. Peel and finely chop the garlic, or pass it through a garlic press.

Place the artichokes, garlic, spinach, mayonnaise, mozzarella, 1/2 cup of the Parmesan, and the onion in a large bowl and stir until well combined. Spoon into an ungreased 8-inch square baking pan and top with the remaining 1/2 cup Parmesan cheese. Bake for 20 to 25 minutes, or until it just begins to bubble on the edges. Serve warm with crackers or pita chips on the side.

Although artichokes are awesome in dips with all kinds of cheesy goodness, they are also great served steamed with butter. To steam whole artichokes, lop off the top of the artichoke with a sharp knife, and snip sharp points off the outer leaves (these are actually petals, because the artichoke is a flower). Place them in a large pan with about an inch of water. Cook for about 20 to 30 minutes over medium-high heat, or until the base of the artichoke is softer and the leaves can be pulled out fairly easily. Drain the water and serve with a dish of melted butter, pulling off and discarding the tough outer leaves, then dipping the bases of the more tender inner leaves into the melted butter and nibbling.

cooking 101

impressing your date

stuffed acorn squash

m: You can prepare this dish mostly in advance—which lets you focus on getting ready for your date rather than fussing around in the kitchen. I'd suggest you serve it with a green salad with balsamic or some other light vinaigrette. **Serves 2**

2 large acorn squash

$1/2$ onion

4 ounces mushrooms

$3/4$ cup ricotta cheese (see Cooking 101, below)

$3/4$ cup grated Swiss cheese

1 egg

$1/2$ teaspoon ground nutmeg

Salt and pepper

$1/4$ cup breadcrumbs

Up to 4 hours before mealtime, cut a small slice off one side of each squash so they'll sit flat. Cut off about one-fourth of the opposite side of the squash (to give you access to the hollow in the middle) and discard. Scrape out the seeds and strings with a spoon.

Peel the onion and cut into $1/8$- to $1/4$-inch pieces. Cut the ends off the mushroom stems, discard, and cut the mushrooms into $1/4$- to $3/8$-inch pieces. Combine the onion, mushrooms, ricotta cheese, Swiss cheese, egg, and nutmeg, and stir well. Season with salt and pepper.

Place the squash in a baking dish, spoon half of the cheese mixture into each squash, then sprinkle the breadcrumbs over the cheese. Cover with plastic wrap and refrigerate until ready to bake.

About $1 1/2$ hours before mealtime, preheat the oven to 375°F. Remove the plastic wrap and bake the squash for 1 hour, or until a fork slides easily into the squash.

Place each squash in a shallow bowl and serve immediately.

You have to do this at least once, so you can nonchalantly say, "I like to make my own ricotta." Heat $1/2$ gallon of whole milk to 200°F, stirring frequently to keep it from scorching. When it reaches 200°F, stir in 2 tablespoons of fresh lemon juice. It will instantly curdle (if it doesn't, keep heating). Remove from the heat and let stand for 5 minutes. Line a colander with a couple layers of cheesecloth and slowly pour in the milk mixture. Allow it to drain until the cheesecloth is cool enough to handle. Gather the ends of the cheesecloth together and tie into a bag. Suspend the bag over the sink and allow to drain for 1 hour, then use or refrigerate.

cooking 101

potato gnocchi with
spicy red pepper sauce

J: The first time I had gnocchi—sort of a cross between pasta and a dumpling—was in Venice, and it was great! So of course I had to try to make my own. Mine weren't as spectacular, but after a few more tries, I got it. The key is to only add enough flour for the dough not to be sticky anymore; otherwise, they'll be too heavy. When you boil them, you can tell whether the dough is okay. If the gnocchi start to feather and fall apart when you boil them, you need more flour. If they don't float after 2 minutes, they have too much flour. This is another dish that works well with a nice green salad. **Serves 2**

Gnocchi

3 russet potatoes (about 1 pound)

1/2 teaspoon salt

1 egg yolk

3/4 cup flour

Sauce

2 red bell peppers

1 onion

1 stalk celery

1 carrot

1 tablespoon canola oil

1 (6-ounce) can tomato paste

1/2 teaspoon crushed red pepper

1/2 cup water

Salt and pepper

3 tablespoons butter

2 ounces crumbled feta cheese

To prepare the gnocchi: Up to 6 hours before mealtime, preheat the oven to 400°F.

Poke several holes in each potato and bake for 45 minutes, or until fairly soft when squeezed. While the potatoes are still hot, cut them in half and squeeze the insides into a bowl, discarding the skins. (You'll want to use a hot pad to do this.) Mash the potato well with a potato masher or a sturdy fork, add the salt and egg yolk to the bowl, and stir well. Add the flour a little at a time and mix with your hands until the mixture just begins to hold together. Transfer the dough to a lightly floured work surface and knead gently for 1 minute, or until smooth. You may need to add a little bit more flour to keep the dough from sticking.

Break off a handful of the dough and roll it into a 1/2-inch-thick rope. Cut the rope into 1-inch pieces. Repeat this process with the remaining dough.

Bring a large saucepan of salted water to a boil and add one-fourth of the gnocchi. Cook for 2 minutes after they float to the surface, then remove with a slotted spoon. Repeat the process with the remaining gnocchi. Place the gnocchi in a single layer in a baking pan or on a large plate, cover with plastic wrap, and refrigerate until ready to use.

To prepare the sauce: Up to 6 hours before mealtime, roast the red peppers by placing each whole pepper directly on the gas stove burner (if you have an electric stove, do this under the broiler) and cook, turning occasionally, for 10 to 15 minutes, or until they are almost completely black. Place them

continued

potato gnocchi with spicy red pepper sauce, continued

Red and green bell peppers are actually the same plant. Green peppers are picked when the peppers are green (go figure) and red peppers are left on the vine longer until they ripen and turn red. The longer time on the vine results in red peppers being sweeter than the green. Choose smooth, firm peppers with no shriveled or soft spots and avoid the heavy ones. They are loaded with seeds.

Feta, which is a salted Greek cheese, can be mild or sharp, soft or hard. In the supermarket you'll find it either as a chunk immersed in brine (it spoils quickly after being taken out of the brine) or already crumbled in a package. Buy the latter for this recipe—any leftover is excellent sprinkled over salad.

in a bowl, cover tightly with plastic wrap, and let stand for 10 minutes. (The steam will make the skins peel right off.) Scrape the blackened skin off the peppers and discard the stems and seeds. Place the pepper in the blender and purée until smooth.

Peel the onion and cut into 1/2-inch pieces. Trim the ends from the celery and cut into 1/4-inch-thick slices. Peel the carrot, cut in half lengthwise, and slice 1/4 inch thick.

Heat the oil in a medium saucepan over medium heat. Add the onion, celery, and carrot, and cook, stirring frequently, for 12 to 15 minutes, or until the vegetables are fairly soft. Add the puréed red peppers, tomato paste, crushed red pepper, and water and stir well. Season with salt and pepper and cool to room temperature. Cover and refrigerate until ready to use.

Thirty minutes before mealtime, remove the gnocchi and sauce from the refrigerator and let stand at room temperature.

Fifteen minutes before mealtime, place the butter in a large skillet over medium heat. Add the gnocchi and cook, stirring occasionally, for 12 to 15 minutes, or until lightly browned on two sides.

Meanwhile, place the sauce over low heat and cook, stirring occasionally, for 10 to 15 minutes, or until hot.

Spoon half of the gnocchi onto each plate and top with the sauce. Sprinkle with the feta cheese and serve immediately.

onion stuffed with quinoa and mushrooms

j: I had never tried quinoa before testing this recipe, and my verdict is that the grain with the funny name is good. The combination of vegetables and quinoa is so delicious that I would be happy with a big bowl of just that. This is even better though, because stuffing it into the onion makes an awesome and impressive dish. **Serves 2**

3/4 cup quinoa

1 vegetable bouillon cube

1 large onion (3 1/2 to 4 inches in diameter)

8 ounces mushrooms

1 carrot

1 stalk celery

2 tablespoons canola oil

Salt and pepper

1 bunch red chard

Up to 6 hours before mealtime, place the quinoa in a stainer and rinse under cold running water for 1 minute. Fill a saucepan with water, add the quinoa and bouillon cube, and bring to a boil. Cover and cook over medium-low heat for 15 minutes, or until the quinoa is tender. Drain in a strainer and set aside.

Peel the onion and cut about 1 inch off the top. Pop out the center of the onion, leaving just the 2 outer layers. (Cut an X in the center few rings of the onion from the top to the bottom

continued

onion stuffed with quinoa and mushrooms, continued

and wiggle the knife around to remove the middle of the onion. It doesn't matter if the center of the onion gets broken up because you are chopping it anyway. Once you have the center out, use your fingers to remove the remaining rings, keeping the 2 outer layers intact.) Chop the inside of the onion into 1/2-inch pieces. Cut the ends off the mushroom stems, discard, and cut the mushrooms into quarters. Peel the carrot, cut in half lengthwise, then cut into 1/4-inch-thick slices. Trim and discard the ends of the celery, cut in half lengthwise, then cut into 1/4-inch-thick slices.

Place the oil in a large skillet over medium-high heat. Add the mushrooms, chopped onion, carrot, and celery and cook, stirring frequently, for 12 to 15 minutes, or until the onion is soft. Stir together the quinoa and mushroom mixture and season with salt and pepper.

Carefully separate the two large onion layers, keeping both intact, and place them in an 8-inch square baking pan. Spoon the quinoa mixture into each of the onion layers and cover with aluminum foil. Refrigerate until ready to use.

Cut the thick red stem out of the red chard leaves and rinse the leaves well. Place the still-wet chard leaves in the skillet and cook over medium heat for 5 to 6 minutes, or until completely wilted. Remove from the heat, cool completely, cover with plastic wrap, and refrigerate until ready to use.

One hour and 15 minutes before mealtime, preheat the oven to 350°F. Leave the aluminum foil on the onion shells and bake for 1 hour, or until the quinoa is warmed through.

Five minutes before mealtime, remove the plastic wrap from the chard and cook over medium-high heat, stirring occasionally, for 5 minutes, or until hot.

Place some of the chard in the center of each plate and, using a spatula to keep in the quinoa, carefully top with a quinoa-filled onion shell. Serve immediately.

cheese fondue

j: This is the best cheese fondue I've ever had—Megan got the recipe when she was in France. You can use most kinds of hard white French or Swiss cheese, but be sure not to use store-bought grated cheese. Those cheeses are tossed in cornstarch so the pieces don't stick together. If you use them in cheese fondue, the cornstarch forms a hard lump in the pan. Note that this recipe uses a cup of wine—it's very French to cook with wine—which is one of the things that makes this fondue classic. **Serves 2**

1 (1-pound) French baguette

2 apples

1 tablespoon lemon juice

1 clove garlic

1 cup white wine

6 ounces grated Emmentaler cheese

6 ounces grated Gruyère cheese

6 ounces grated Comté cheese

One hour before mealtime, cut the bread into 1-inch cubes, place in a serving bowl, and cover tightly with plastic wrap. Cut each of the apples into 8 wedges, remove the cores, and cut each wedge in half crosswise. Place the apples in a bowl and sprinkle with the lemon juice. Add enough cold water to cover the apples and refrigerate until ready to use. (Holding the apples in water with lemon juice keeps them from browning.)

Fifteen minutes before mealtime, peel the garlic, cut it in half, and rub the cut sides over the bottom of a saucepan. Pour the wine into the pan and bring to a boil over medium heat. Add the cheeses and cook, stirring frequently, for 10 to 12 minutes, or until the cheese is melted. (The wine will not be completely incorporated into the cheese. Some of it will stay on top of the cheese.) Pour the fondue into a serving bowl.

Drain the apples and serve immediately with the bread and hot fondue. Spear a piece of bread or apple on a fork, dip it into the fondue, and eat.

> **They say necessity is the mother of invention, and that holds true here in a very tasty way.** In the 1700s cheese was central to the diet of most Swiss villagers, because it could be made in the summer to last through the winter months. The Swiss found that heating stale cheese over a fire improved the taste and made it much easier to eat, and that hard bread would soften when dipped into the melted cheese. They soon learned that mixing in wine and other seasonings made it even better, transforming old cheese and bread into a flavorful meal.
>
> **food trivia**

mushroom ravioli in browned butter

m: Here we came up with a new way to do ravioli with wonton wrappers. It's quick and simple but looks impressive and tastes like what you'd get in a five-star restaurant. The ravioli are sautéed in butter and sprinkled with Parmesan cheese. It does not get much better than that. Serve it with (what else?) green salad and some rustic Italian bread like ciabatta. **Serves 2**

Oil or cooking spray

4 ounces portobello, shiitake, or other brown mushrooms

1/2 small onion

1 tablespoon canola oil

Salt and pepper

20 (3-inch) wonton wrappers

3 tablespoons butter

1/4 cup grated Parmesan cheese

1 tablespoon chopped fresh parsley

When buying mushrooms, look for firm, smooth mushrooms that are dry but not dried out. Keep mushrooms in their original packaging for up to a week in the refrigerator, but once you've opened the package, store them in a paper bag in the fridge. Most important, keep them dry, because moisture makes them spoil quickly.

cooking 101

Up to 4 hours before mealtime, lightly coat a baking sheet with oil or cooking spray. Cut the ends off the mushroom stems, discard, and cut the mushrooms into very thin slices. Peel the onion and cut into 1/4-inch pieces.

Place the oil in a skillet over medium heat. Add the mushrooms and onion and cook, stirring frequently, for 12 to 15 minutes, or until the onion is soft and all the liquid is evaporated. Season with salt and pepper.

Lay a wonton wrapper on a work surface, dip your finger in water, and wet the entire edge of the wrapper. Place a spoonful of the mushroom mixture in the center and top with another wonton wrapper. Firmly press the edges to seal, and just before you seal it completely, push gently around the filling to remove any air pockets. Repeat the process with the remaining ingredients. Lay the finished ravioli on a baking sheet, keeping them separate so they don't stick together.

Bring a large pot of salted water to a boil. Carefully lower a few of the ravioli into the water using a slotted spoon and cook for 2 to 3 minutes, or until the wrapper is translucent. Remove with the slotted spoon, drain well, and place on the baking sheet. Lay a sheet of plastic wrap right on top of the ravioli, smoothing it down to remove any air pockets. Refrigerate until ready to use.

Fifteen minutes before mealtime, place the butter in a large saucepan and cook over medium heat for 5 minutes, or until browned. Add the ravioli to the pan one at a time, making sure each is thoroughly coated in butter before adding another. (If they aren't coated with butter, they'll stick together and tear when you try to separate them.) Cook for 8 to 10 minutes, or until warm. Spoon the ravioli onto plates, sprinkle with the Parmesan cheese and parsley, and serve immediately.

coconut-lime curry

m : One day I was looking through my cupboard trying to decide what I would have for dinner and came upon a can of coconut milk. The truth is, I only bought it because it sounded fun and exotic, but I had no idea what to make with it. After a little more digging I came up with the coconut-curry combination and the rest, as they say, is history. All right, that might be a little bit of an exaggeration, but it is very tasty—definitely impress-your-date material. **Serves 2**

4 ounces rice noodles

1/2 red bell pepper

1/2 yellow bell pepper

1 small onion

1 carrot

2 cloves garlic

1 tablespoon canola oil

1 cup coconut milk

1/4 cup lime juice

1 teaspoon curry powder

2 tablespoons chopped cilantro

Coconut milk is made by soaking and squeezing grated coconut meat. It is much thicker and richer than coconut water (coconut juice), which is found inside the hollow of the coconut. Whatever you do, buy regular (full fat) coconut milk. This is one of those cases where the low-fat version is not worth using.

cooking 101

Up to 3 hours before mealtime, bring a large saucepan of salted water to a boil and add the rice noodles. Cook over medium-high heat, stirring occasionally, for 10 minutes, or until al dente. Drain the noodles in a colander and rinse with cold water. Place the noodles in a resealable bag and refrigerate until ready to use.

Remove the seeds and membranes from the bell peppers, then cut the peppers into thin slices. Peel the onion and cut into thin slices. Peel the carrot, then cut into thin slices on the diagonal. Peel and finely chop the garlic or pass it through a garlic press.

Heat the oil in a large skillet over medium-high heat. Add the bell peppers, onion, carrot, and garlic and cook, stirring frequently, for 12 to 15 minutes, or until the onion is translucent and the peppers are beginning to get soft. Remove from the heat and let cool. Cover and refrigerate until ready to use.

Fifteen minutes before mealtime, place the pan with the peppers over medium heat and cook for 2 minutes, or until the peppers begin to warm up. Add the coconut milk, lime juice, and curry powder and cook for 4 to 5 minutes, or until the sauce just begins to bubble. Add the rice noodles and stir until thoroughly coated. Cook for 4 to 5 minutes, or until the noodles are warm.

Spoon the noodles onto plates, making sure there are some pieces of pepper and carrot on top. Sprinkle with the cilantro and serve immediately.

butternut squash risotto

m : We use vegetable bouillon cubes to add to the flavor in a lot of our recipes, and they really make all the difference here, adding body and depth to this risotto. Don't get too concerned about size when you are cutting up the butternut squash. If you have different-sized pieces the smaller ones will soften as they cook and mix in, enhancing the creaminess, and the larger pieces will retain their shape, giving the risotto more texture.

Serves 2

1 small butternut squash (about 1 pound)

1/2 small onion

2 tablespoons butter

1/2 cup Arborio rice

1 vegetable bouillon cube

2 1/2 cups hot water

Salt and pepper

1/4 cup grated Parmesan cheese

Up to 2 hours before mealtime, cut the butternut squash into chunks and remove and discard the peel and seeds. Cut into 1/4- to 1/2-inch chunks. Peel the onion and cut into 1/2-inch pieces.

Place the butter in a skillet over medium-high heat. Add the onion and cook, stirring frequently, for 12 to 15 minutes, or until the onion is translucent. Add the squash and Arborio rice and stir well. Place the bouillon cube in the water and smash it with a fork to break it up a little, then pour 1/4 cup of the water into the pan and cook over medium heat, stirring constantly, until all the liquid has been absorbed. Continue adding the water, 1/4 cup at a time, until you've used 1 3/4 cups of the water. It will take about 30 minutes to get to this point. Remove from the heat, cover, and let stand.

Twenty minutes before mealtime, stir 1/2 cup of the water into the risotto and cook over medium heat, stirring constantly, for 8 to 10 minutes, or until the water is completely absorbed. Repeat the process with the remaining 1/4 cup of water.

Season with salt and pepper, spoon the risotto onto plates, sprinkle with the Parmesan cheese, and serve immediately.

Risotto is usually made with Arborio rice because it has a very high starch content (Carnaroli and Vialone Nano are the other good risotto rices). The starch gets released as you gradually stir in hot liquid, resulting in a creamy texture that you just can't get with regular white rice.

cooking 101

fettuccine with mushroom bolognese sauce

j: This is a very safe (and, of course, tasty) pasta dish guaranteed to please those less adventurous eaters. It is also good for you less-experienced cooks. It really is simple to make and almost impossible to ruin. **Serves 2**

8 ounces fettuccine

1/2 onion

1 carrot

4 ounces mushrooms

1 tablespoon olive oil

Salt and pepper

1 (15-ounce) can tomato sauce

1/2 teaspoon Italian seasoning

1 tablespoon sugar

2 tablespoons grated Parmesan cheese

Up to 5 hours before mealtime, bring a large pot of salted water to a boil and add the fettuccine. Cook over medium-high heat, stirring occasionally, for 12 minutes, or until al dente. Drain in a colander and rinse under cold water. Place in a resealable bag and refrigerate until ready to use.

Peel the onion and cut into 1/2-inch pieces. Peel the carrot, cut in half lengthwise, and slice 1/4 inch thick. Remove and discard the mushroom stems and thinly slice. Heat the oil in a medium saucepan over medium heat. Add the onion, carrot, and mushrooms and cook, stirring occasionally, for 12 to 15 minutes, or until the mushrooms are golden and the juices have evaporated. Season with salt and pepper and add the tomato sauce, Italian seasoning, and sugar. Cook for 15 to 20 minutes, or until slightly thickened. Cool to room temperature, cover, and refrigerate until ready to use.

Fifteen minutes before mealtime, place the sauce over medium heat and cook for 8 to 10 minutes, or until hot. Bring a saucepan of water to a boil. Add the fettuccine and cook for 1 minute, or until warm.

Place half of the pasta onto each plate and top with half of the sauce. Sprinkle the Parmesan cheese over the pasta and serve immediately.

Fresh mushrooms should be brushed off, rinsed briefly under running water, and patted dry with a paper towel. Never soak them in water; they are like little sponges and will absorb water and become soggy.

cooking 101

vegan cheesecake

j: I know I continually say that I'm skeptical about tofu, especially something as weird as tofu cream cheese. However, I have to say this vegan cheesecake is actually better than a lot of cheesecakes I've had. In fact, it's so good that when I finished my first piece I went back for a second. Like any cheesecake, it's great with any kind of fruit on top, especially strawberries. **Serves 6**

1 1/2 cups graham cracker crumbs

1/4 cup firmly packed brown sugar

1/4 cup melted margarine

24 ounces soy cream cheese

3/4 cup granulated sugar

3/4 cup egg substitute

2 teaspoons vanilla extract

Preheat the oven to 325°F.

Stir together the graham cracker crumbs, brown sugar, and margarine in an ungreased 9-inch pie pan and press down to cover the bottom and sides of the pan.

Place the cream cheese in a bowl and stir until smooth. Add the granulated sugar, egg substitute, and vanilla and stir until completely combined. Pour the mixture into the crust and bake for 30 minutes. Turn down the oven to 250°F and bake for 20 to 30 minutes, or until set in the center. Remove from the oven and cool completely before serving.

You can save several dollars by buying a box of graham crackers and smashing them up yourself. Just put them in a plastic bag and smash them with a rolling pin or the bottom of a heavy pan. Or you can give them a whirl in a food processor if you have one. It takes about 15 graham crackers to yield 1 1/2 cups.

bargain shopper

chocolate cake

j: This type of cake recipe—using oil, not butter, and without eggs—was first developed during the Depression era, when milk and eggs were scarce and expensive. Rather than forgo sweets entirely, families developed recipes that worked around the limited availability of certain foods. Obviously, the availability of dairy isn't an issue anymore, but this history means that there are plenty of pretty good dessert recipes ready-made for vegans. **Serves 12**

Oil or cooking spray

3 cups flour

2 cups sugar

$^1/_2$ cup unsweetened cocoa powder

2 teaspoons baking soda

1 teaspoon salt

$^2/_3$ cup canola oil

2 teaspoons vanilla extract

2 teaspoons white vinegar

2 cups water

2 cups coarsely chopped pecans

Preheat the oven to 350°F. Lightly coat a 9 by 13-inch baking pan with oil or cooking spray.

Stir together the flour, sugar, cocoa, baking soda, and salt. Make a well, or funnel-shaped indentation, in the center of the dry ingredients and add the oil, vanilla, vinegar, and water. Stir until smooth. Pour the batter into the prepared pan and sprinkle with the pecans. Bake for 40 to 45 minutes, or until a toothpick inserted into the center comes out clean.

The Aztecs first prepared a hot chocolate drink for a European in 1519. It was then introduced to the Spanish court in 1528, and it gradually spread through Europe. However, chocolate wasn't prepared for eating until 1765, when it was made at Milton Lower Mills, near present-day Dorchester, Massachusetts.

food trivia

tofu pumpkin pie

m : This is a recipe that I first tried out a really long time ago for a friend in high school who had decided to become a vegan. A pie with tofu may sound odd, but silken tofu is very smooth when you blend it, and helps make vegan desserts rich and satisfying without dairy products. Although the texture is a little different than traditional pumpkin pie, the taste is almost exactly the same. The only way to make this better is to find vegan whipped cream to put on top. **Serves 6**

1 prepared piecrust (see page 5)

16 ounces silken tofu

1 (30-ounce) can pumpkin purée

1 1/2 cups sugar

2 tablespoons pumpkin pie spice

1 teaspoon salt

Pumpkin pie's primitive cousin, pumpkin pudding, originated with the early American colonists in New England. They sliced off the top of a pumpkin and removed the seeds. They then filled the inside with milk, spices, and honey and baked it in hot ashes.

food trivia

Preheat the oven to 425°F. Press the piecrust into an ungreased 8-inch pie pan.

Place the tofu, pumpkin, sugar, pumpkin pie spice, and salt in a blender and pulse until smooth. (You may have to stop the blender and push down the ingredients a couple of times.) Pour the mixture into the piecrust and bake for 15 minutes. Turn down the oven to 350°F and continue to bake for 20 to 25 minutes, or until the pie filling is set in the center. Remove from the oven and cool completely before serving.

vegan raspberry-almond bread pudding

m : I love bread pudding, but making it without any dairy was a bit of a challenge. After quite a few attempts, we finally got it. This version is not too sweet, and the combination of almond milk and raspberries gives it an excellent flavor. **Serves 4**

Oil or cooking spray

10 slices day-old bread

2 cups almond milk

$1/3$ cup sugar

1 teaspoon cinnamon

1 cup fresh or frozen raspberries

Preheat the oven to 375°F. Lightly coat a 9-inch baking pan with oil or cooking spray.

Cut the bread into $1/2$- to $3/4$-inch cubes and place in the prepared pan. Combine the almond milk, sugar, and cinnamon in a bowl and pour over the bread. Add the raspberries to the pan and stir until just combined. Bake for 45 to 50 minutes, or until the center is set.

? Almond milk is made from grinding almonds and water. It's easier to buy it, but if you wanted, you could actually make it at home. Unlike cow's or goat's milk, it doesn't have any cholesterol, and it's also free of lactose. It was widely used in Europe, the Middle East, and into Asia in the Middle Ages, for a number of reasons, not least because animal milk wouldn't keep for long without spoiling, so it was usually immediately made into butter or cheese.

food trivia

peach pie with crumble topping

m: We can't write a cookbook without including something with a crumble topping; they're just too good. That's why we came up with this vegan version of crumble, which wasn't even really that hard (all we had to do was change the butter to margarine—so if you want to make a dairy version, switch back to butter). Serve a nice warm slice with a scoop of ice cream (vegan if you like) and you'll be in heaven! **Serves 6**

1 prepared piecrust (see page 5)

2 (29-ounce) cans sliced peaches

1 cup granulated sugar

1/4 cup cornstarch

2 tablespoons lemon juice

1/2 cup margarine or butter

1/2 cup brown sugar

1 cup flour

1/2 teaspoon cinnamon

Preheat the oven to 375°F. Press the piecrust into an ungreased 9-inch pie pan.

Drain the peaches and place in a large bowl. Sprinkle with the granulated sugar, cornstarch, and lemon juice and stir until fairly well combined. Pour the peaches into the pie pan and spread them out evenly.

Place the margarine, brown sugar, flour, and cinnamon in a bowl and mix with a fork, mashing together until crumbly. Spoon the mixture evenly over the peaches and bake for 55 to 60 minutes, or until the top is golden brown. Serve warm or at room temperature.

> **One of the first recipes for pie dough appears in a cookbook from 1545 called *A Proper newe Booke of Cokerye, declarynge what maner of meates be beste in season, for al times in the yere, and how they ought to be dressed, and serued at the table, bothe for fleshe dayes, and fyshe day.* The recipe reads, "To make short paest for tarte. Take fyne floure and a cursey of fayre water and a dysche of swete butter and a lyttel saffron, and the yolckes of two egges and make it thynne and as tender as ye maye."**
>
> **food trivia**

vegan chocolate pudding

m : This recipe, which is as easy as one, two, three, is great for that late-night sweet tooth because it's so quick to make. We tried it out with every kind of nondairy milk possible and they all worked, but this was our favorite. **Serves 4**

1/3 cup sugar

1/4 cup unsweetened cocoa powder

1/4 cup cornstarch

Pinch of salt

3 cups soymilk

Combine the sugar, cocoa, cornstarch, and salt in a saucepan and slowly stir in the soymilk. Cook over medium heat, stirring constantly, for 10 minutes, or until it comes to a boil. Cook for 1 more minute and remove from the heat. Pour into individual bowls and refrigerate until completely chilled.

In the late 1800s some American social reformers and food companies promoted puddings as health foods, touting their nutritional benefits to invalids and children. If they add college students to that group, I'm all for bringing back that campaign.

food trivia

cinnamon sugar cookies

J: The best way to describe these tasty cookies is like giant cinnamon Teddy Grahams. You could even make them look like little bears, but that's only if you have way too much time on your hands. You can bake them to suit your tastes: if you like softer cookies, take them out on the early side; if you like crunchy cookies, leave them in for the full 10 minutes. **Makes about 36 cookies**

1 cup softened margarine or butter

1/2 cup granulated sugar

1/2 cup firmly packed brown sugar

2 cups flour

1 tablespoon cinnamon

1/2 teaspoon baking soda

Preheat the oven to 325°F.

Place the margarine, granulated sugar, and brown sugar in a large bowl and stir vigorously until smooth and creamy. Add the flour, cinnamon, and baking soda and stir until thoroughly combined.

Drop heaping teaspoonfuls of the dough about 2 inches apart onto ungreased cookie sheets. Bake for 8 to 10 minutes, or until lightly browned on the edges.

Baking soda and baking powder are both leavening agents, which means they cause baked goods to rise, but they're used in different situations. To be effective, baking soda must be combined with acidic ingredients. This causes carbon dioxide bubbles to form, which raises the dough. Baking powder contains everything it needs to raise dough when combined with liquid ingredients, so it can be used in recipes that don't include acidic ingredients. And sometimes both are used.

cooking 101

fried ice cream

m : Okay, this isn't really fried (which is a good thing), but the crunchy cinnamon crust with cold, creamy ice cream inside does a good job of imitating fried ice cream. It's so delicious that everyone will be asking for seconds. Make it to share with friends, and keep it in your freezer in a covered container to eat whenever you get sick of boring, plain old ice cream out of the carton. To make a vegan version, use margarine and nondairy ice cream. **Serves 9**

1/4 cup melted margarine or butter

1/4 cup firmly packed brown sugar

1 cup crumbled cornflakes

1/4 cup shredded coconut

1/4 cup chopped pecans

2 tablespoons cinnamon

2 quarts nondairy or regular vanilla ice cream, slightly softened

Chocolate sauce (optional)

Place the margarine, brown sugar, cornflake crumbs, coconut, pecans, and cinnamon in a bowl and stir until combined. Spread half of the mixture in the bottom of an ungreased 8-inch square baking pan. Carefully spread the ice cream over the crumb mixture, keeping the crumbs intact. Spread the remaining crumb mixture over the ice cream and press firmly.

Freeze until firm before serving. Cut into 9 squares and drizzle with chocolate sauce, if desired.

cherry turnovers

J: These turnovers are delicious! Plus, they're quick to make and everyone loves them. When you're making them, be sure to put only a few cherries and a little bit of sauce in each one; otherwise, they'll be really hard to close and they'll leak all over the place. **Makes 8 turnovers**

Oil or cooking spray

2 cups frozen pitted cherries

$1/2$ cup water

$1/4$ cup sugar, plus extra for dusting

1 tablespoon cornstarch

2 sheets puff pastry, thawed (see page 5)

Preheat the oven to 400°F. Lightly coat a baking sheet with oil or cooking spray.

Place the cherries, $1/4$ cup of the water, and the $1/4$ cup of sugar in a saucepan and cook over medium heat for 10 minutes, or until it comes to a boil. In a small bowl, combine the cornstarch and the remaining $1/4$ cup of water, mix until smooth, then stir into the pan. Cook for 2 minutes, or until it comes to a boil. Remove from the heat and cool slightly.

Lay each puff pastry sheet flat and cut into quarters. Spoon some of the cherry mixture into the center of each pastry square. Wet your finger and dampen the entire edge of the puff pastry squares. Fold each square over to form a triangle and press gently to seal the edges. Brush the top with a little water and sprinkle with sugar. Place the turnovers on the prepared baking sheet and bake for 20 to 25 minutes, or until golden brown.

> **Cherries, both sweet and sour, originated in eastern Europe and western Asia, and that region still produces most of the cherries in the world. In the United States (also a big cherry-producing nation), sweet cherries are grown mostly in California, Oregon, and Washington; Michigan produces most of our sour cherries.**
>
> **food trivia**

pecan phyllo spirals

m: We use phyllo dough in this recipe to make a tasty little dessert that is almost like mini baklavas. They're perfect for parties because you can pick them up easily and they aren't messy. The only problem is, you'll have to make lots because they go like hotcakes! **Makes 36 spirals**

2 cups chopped pecans

$^1/_2$ cup sugar

2 teaspoons cinnamon

12 sheets phyllo dough, thawed (see page 5)

$^1/_3$ cup melted margarine or butter

$^1/_2$ cup honey

$^1/_4$ cup orange juice

Preheat the oven to 400°F.

Combine the pecans, sugar, and cinnamon in a bowl.

Unroll the phyllo dough, place on a flat surface, and separate out a stack of 12 sheets, gently lifting them off as a single unit. Cover the 12 sheets of phyllo with barely damp paper towels. (Be sure to cover the phyllo every time you take a sheet or it will dry out.) Return the remaining dough to its packaging, seal tightly, and refrigerate or freeze, depending on how soon you'll use it. Place a sheet of phyllo on a flat surface and brush with melted margarine. Continue the layering process with sheets of phyllo brushed with margarine until you have 4 phyllo sheets in the stack. Sprinkle one-third of the nut mixture over the phyllo dough, covering the entire surface, then roll the phyllo up tightly lengthwise, and brush with margarine. Place the roll seam side down, cut it into $^3/_4$- to 1-inch pieces, and place the rolls flat in an ungreased 9 by 13-inch baking pan. Repeat the process with the remaining ingredients. Bake for 15 to 20 minutes, or until golden brown.

Combine the honey and orange juice in a small bowl, stir until well combined, then pour the mixture over the rolls. Serve warm or at room temperature.

I love cinnamon . . . or I thought I did. The name *cinnamon* refers to cinnamon from a tree grown in Ceylon; however, a related species, *Cassia*, is also often sold labeled as cinnamon. So even if you think you're buying real cinnamon, most of the powdered cinnamon sold in stores in the U.S. is actually cassia. But don't start screaming fraud just yet—they're very similar, with cassia just being stronger in flavor than cinnamon.

food trivia

index